Embracing Our Finitude

VERITAS
Series Introduction

"... the truth will set you free" (John 8:32)

In much contemporary discourse, Pilate's question has been taken to mark the absolute boundary of human thought. Beyond this boundary, it is often suggested, is an intellectual hinterland into which we must not venture. This terrain is an agnosticism of thought: because truth cannot be possessed, it must not be spoken. Thus, it is argued that the defenders of "truth" in our day are often traffickers in ideology, merchants of counterfeits, or anti-liberal. They are, because it is somewhat taken for granted that Nietzsche's word is final: truth is the domain of tyranny.

Is this indeed the case, or might another vision of truth offer itself? The ancient Greeks named the love of wisdom as *philia*, or friendship. The one who would become wise, they argued, would be a "friend of truth." For both philosophy and theology might be conceived as schools in the friendship of truth, as a kind of relation. For like friendship, truth is as much discovered as it is made. If truth is then so elusive, if its domain is *terra incognita*, perhaps this is because it arrives to us—unannounced—as gift, as a person, and not some thing.

The aim of the Veritas book series is to publish incisive and original current scholarly work that inhabits "the between" and "the beyond" of theology and philosophy. These volumes will all share a common aspiration to transcend the institutional divorce in which these two disciplines often find themselves, and to engage questions of pressing concern to both philosophers and theologians in such a way as to reinvigorate both disciplines with a kind of interdisciplinary desire, often so absent in contemporary academe. In a word, these volumes represent collective efforts in the befriending of truth, doing so beyond the simulacra of pretend tolerance, the violent, yet insipid reasoning of liberalism that asks with Pilate, "What is truth?"—expecting a consensus of non-commitment; one that encourages the commodification of the mind, now sedated by the civil service of career, ministered by the frightened patrons of position.

The series will therefore consist of two "wings": (1) original monographs; and (2) essay collections on a range of topics in theology and philosophy. The latter will principally be the products of the annual conferences of the Centre of Theology and Philosophy (www.theologyphilosophycentre .co.uk).

Conor Cunningham and Eric Austin Lee, *Series editors*

Embracing Our Finitude

Exercises in a Christian Anthropology between
Dependence and Gratitude

STEPHAN KAMPOWSKI

CASCADE *Books* · Eugene, Oregon

EMBRACING OUR FINITUDE
Exercises in a Christian Anthropology between Dependence and Gratitude

Veritas 29

Cascade Books
An Imprint of Wipf and Stock Publishers
199 W. 8th Ave., Suite 3
Eugene, OR 97401

www.wipfandstock.com

PAPERBACK ISBN: 978-1-5326-1889-5
HARDCOVER ISBN: 978-1-4982-4476-3
EBOOK ISBN: 978-1-4982-4475-6

Cataloguing-in-Publication data:

Names: Kampowski, Stephan, author.

Title: Embracing our finitude : exercises in a Christian anthropology between dependence and gratitude / Stephan Kampowski.

Description: Eugene, OR : Cascade Books, 2018 | Series: Veritas 29 | Includes bibliographical references and index.

Identifiers: ISBN 978-1-5326-1889-5 (paperback) | ISBN 978-1-4982-4476-3 (hardcover) | ISBN 978-1-4982-4475-6 (ebook)

Subjects: LCSH: Theological anthropology. | Finite, The. | Gratitude—Religious aspects—Christianity. | Dependency.

Classification: BD411 .K36 2018 (print) | BD411 .K36 (ebook)

Manufactured in the U.S.A.   05/15/18

To Livio Melina

Contents

Credits

With three exceptions, the essays contained in this volume are published here in English for the first time. In what follows, the places of their first publication are indicated. Grateful acknowledgment is made to the editors and publishers who have kindly granted permission to include the texts in this book where permission was necessary. All essays have originally been written in English. They have undergone small revisions.

Chapter 1, "Dependence and Gratitude," was first published as *Contingenza creaturale e gratitudine*. Siena: Cantagalli, 2012.

Chapter 2, "Judgment and Common Sense," was first published as "Is There a Saving Judgment?" *Anthropotes* 30 (2014) 579–608.

Chapter 3, "On Why We Act: The Question of Teleology," was first published as "La teleologia dell'azione e la comunione tra gli uomini." In *Persona e natura nell'agire morale*, edited by Juan José Pérez-Soba and Pawel Gałuszka, 277–94. Siena: Cantagalli, 2013.

Chapter 4, "Intercultural Dialogue and God's Project for the Family: Dogma, Culture, and History" was first published under the same title in *Anthropotes* 31 (2015) 361–77.

Chapter 5, "A Promise to Keep: Which Bond, Whose Fidelity?," was first published under the same title in *Anthropotes* 30 (2014) 187–215.

Chapter 6, "The Universal and the Concrete—an Order for Love?," was first published as "Universalità e concretezza: un ordine per l'amore?" In *Il logos dell'agape. Amore e ragione come principi dell'agire*, edited by Juan José Pérez-Soba and Luis Granados, 193–203. Siena: Cantagalli, 2008.

Chapter 7, "Building the Kingdom on Earth? Evangelical Zeal and the Utopian Temptation," was first published as "Migliorare il mondo o diventare buoni? Il dilemma della prassi." In *Primato del Vangelo e luogo della morale: gerarchia e unità nella proposta cristiana*, edited by Juan José Pérez-Soba and Juan Justo de la Torre, 243–55. Siena: Cantagalli, 2015.

Chapter 8, "Love of the Common Good: The Principle of Social Life," was first published as "Amore e vita sociale." In *L'amore principio di vita sociale: "Caritas aedificat" (1Cor 8,1)*, edited by Juan José Pérez-Soba and Mojca Magdic, 203–17. Siena: Cantagalli, 2011.

Chapter 9, "*Ab Urbe Condita:* Arendt and Authority," was first published as "Per che cosa vale la pena di esistere? Il rapporto tra autorità e responsabilità." *Liberal* 38 (2006) 92–97.

Introduction

MEMENTO MORI—REMEMBER DEATH—THIS IS how the medieval monks exhorted us, using a formula that goes back to the times of ancient Rome. Reflecting on this admonition, we may actually marvel at the strange fact that indeed we need to be thus admonished. On the one hand, there is little more obvious than our mortality, while on the other there are few facts of life that we manage to hide better from our consciousness. It seems that for the greater part of our lives, most of us are immersed in the mode of existence that Martin Heidegger calls "*das Man*" or "the they."[1] We keep so busy with superficial everyday chores that we forget that our lives will have an end. In this way, we live in an inauthentic way, just as if we never had to die. For Heidegger, *Dasein,* human existence, becomes truly authentic only in confrontation with death, i.e., in its "being-toward-death," which alone can save human life from shallowness and ensure its authenticity.[2]

It is true: remembering our death makes us see things in perspective. It obliges us to ask about the meaning of our activities. Will they continue to have a meaning once we will have passed from this life? Is there a significance that outlasts us? What is really worth doing? Recalling the fact that we will have to die, we appreciate the value of our time, and it is a millennial wisdom that the habit of counting our days teaches us the wisdom of heart (see Ps 90:12).

1. See Heidegger, *Being and Time*, 118–22 (§27).

2. See ibid., 283 (§62): "One's own potentiality-of-being becomes authentic and transparent in the understanding being-toward-death as the *ownmost* possibility" (original emphasis).

However, there is also the undoubtable fact that thinking about our death provokes a great fear or even anguish in us, as Heidegger himself quite readily admits: "Being-toward-death is essentially *Angst*."[3] To be afraid of dying is connatural to us, independent even of our convictions about what will happen thereafter. Also a believer—convinced that for God's faithful life is changed, not ended—will naturally fear death. This is also the reason why the church considers martyrdom—the testimony to the faith with one's own blood—a heroic act for which one needs a special grace. Fear, in turn, is at the root, perhaps not of all the evils, but certainly of a great many of the evils that we do. If human beings hurt or even kill each other, very often the reason they do so is that they are afraid of each other, perceiving the other as an intruder, a probable villain, and a potential threat. If the peoples wage war, more often than not at the basis there will be one nation's fear of the other. There are even reports of people committing suicide on account of their fear of impending death.

Is there a way of confronting this fear—a fear that at times risks taking away our serenity and joy—without falling back into a superficiality that simply refuses to look reality in the eye? Is there a way of getting reconciled with our mortality? Following the intuitions of Hannah Arendt, I would like to propose that it is important also to keep in mind the other term of the arch of our life, that is, our birth, taking seriously the observation made by Arendt's teacher Heidegger, who notices that death "is just one of the ends that embraces the totality of Da-sein. But the other 'end' is the 'beginning,' 'birth.'"[4] In fact, in a very intriguing passage in her *The Life of the Mind*, Arendt proposes the idea of defining human beings "not, like the Greeks, as mortals, but as 'natals.'"[5] Even though human persons need to die, they "are not born in order to die but in order to begin."[6] In other words, death does not define human life completely. There is not only the end, but also the beginning of life; there is birth. In virtue of birth every human being is a new beginning, called to set new beginnings in time through his or her action. The "natals" do not primarily live *toward* death but *from* birth.

But what could it mean to be "living from birth"? Arendt expresses it very well in a letter addressed to her friend Mary McCarthy, from which we will still have the opportunity to cite once more in the first chapter. To

3. Ibid., 245 (§53).
4. Ibid., 342 (§72).
5. See Arendt, "Willing," in *The Life of the Mind*, 109.
6. Arendt, *Human Condition*, 246.

describe the death of a common friend, McCarthy's partner had used the word "hateful." Arendt responds with these notable and profound words:

> Mary, look, I think I know how sad you are and how serious this loss is. . . . Still—if you just say "hateful" you will have to say hateful to many more things if you want to be consistent. One could look upon one's whole life as a being-given *and* being-taken away. . . . I looked up once more the Jewish death prayers: they, that is, the *kaddish,* are a single praise of God, the name of the dead one is not even mentioned: The underlying notion is what is inscribed on all Jewish funeral homes: The Lord hath given, the Lord hath taken away, blessed be the Lord. Or: Don't complain if something is taken away that was given you but which you did not necessarily *own.* And don't forget, to be taken away, it had first to be given. If you believed you owned, if you forgot that it was given, that is just too bad for you.[7]

Here remembering birth will mean recalling that life, in order to be taken, first needed to be given. It means attending to the gift that we have received, accepting it with gratitude, reminding ourselves that we have not made ourselves. Our life is not something that belongs to us. In her revised doctoral dissertation, Arendt proposes that this remembrance is related to a sense of gratitude and ultimately calms the fear of death.[8]

Remembering birth will also mean bringing to mind the fact that we have received our life within the context of human relations—we live as originally connected to others and never as isolated individuals. Even if Heidegger claims that the human person stands alone before death,[9] the words of the Apostle Paul seem truer to reality: "None of us lives to himself, and none of us dies to himself" (Rom 14:7). As our birth is not a moment in which we are isolated, so neither is our death, which concerns everyone who has ever loved us. But it is particularly birth that tells us that we are not alone. We are inserted into a family and hence into a lineage: we have a father and a mother, grandparents and great-grandparents. We come from others. Here Arendt speaks of the "tremendous bliss that man was created with the power of procreation, that not a single man

---

7. Arendt and McCarthy, *Between Friends,* 307 (original emphases).

8. See Arendt, *Love and Saint Augustine,* 52: "What ultimately stills the fear of death is not hope nor desire, but remembrance and gratitude."

9. See Heidegger, *Being and Time,* 223 (§47): "Every Da-sein must itself actually take dying upon itself. Insofar as it 'is,' death is always essentially my own. . . . In dying, it becomes evident that death is ontologically constituted by mineness and existence."

but Men inhabit the earth."[10] We have an origin that precedes us. Here are the reasons for our existence.[11]

Our mortality and—to use Arendt's term—our "natality" speak to us of the still more general fact that our life is limited; we are finite beings. The chapters of this volume can be seen as a single reflection on this very basic state of affairs. Going beyond recommending a sober and perhaps regretful acknowledgment of human contingency, they propose that we, as human beings, actively embrace our finiteness, recognize our dependency, and respond with gratitude for what has been given to us. Gratitude for the given: this is at the basis of a Christian anthropology as I would like to develop it in the pages that follow.

The chapters are located on the threshold between philosophy and theology. While in general the argumentation itself is intended to be philosophical, a number of times the subject matters will presuppose some very basic truths of revelation: that God exists, that he has created us, that he has revealed himself as love and wants our good. A couple of issues will be of particular concern for the church and her mission, such as the question of judgment, of intercultural dialogue, and of the utopian temptation to build the kingdom on earth.

The volume itself is divided into two parts. The first four chapters deal with the fundamental fact that some things in life are given. They discuss our possible responses to our lack of self-sufficiency (chapter 1) and also reflect on what meaning it may or may not have to speak of human nature. Human nature is presupposed in our judgment (chapter 2) and in our action (chapter 3), inasmuch as the former is based on criteria and the latter is teleological, i.e., oriented to an end. Finally, we will point out that the existence of different cultures is not an argument against human nature, making the case that one can only speak of culture if there is a nature that can be cultivated in the first place (chapter 4).

The second part of this volume deals with the social repercussions of our finitude. A very concrete way of embracing our original dependence on others is to bind ourselves to them by mutual promises (chapter 5). The

---

10. Arendt, "Concluding Remarks," 439.

11. It is possible to correlate Arendt's discourse about "natality" with her juvenile reflections on the createdness of human beings who are in search for the reasons of their existence, which are ultimately found in their origin in the Creator. For the notion of createdness: see Arendt, *Love and Saint Augustine*, 45–97. For the plausible correspondence between "natality" and "createdness" see Kampowski, *Arendt, Augustine and the New Beginning*, 201–9.

following two chapters deal with the utopian temptation to refuse our finiteness, either by depreciating the concrete in the name of the universal, i.e., by loving humanity and forgetting about concrete humans (chapter 6), or by seeking to build the kingdom of God on earth, trying to construct perfect structures while failing to address the human heart (chapter 7). Our finitude, which is expressed in our original relatedness and interdependence, finds a very important manifestation in the question about the true good of the human being. What is the kind of good life—what is the kind of happiness—that is proper to "mortals" who are also "natals"? I will argue that to answer this question in a meaningful way, one needs to look at the notion of the common good (chapter 8). Finally, if Aristotle's insight remains valid, and the human being is indeed a political being who comes to his or her flourishing only in the context of a community's common life, then the problem of authority will be pertinent as a crucial element that holds a community together (chapter 9).

A good number of these essays were written for the yearly conferences organized by the International Research Area on Moral Theology, which is a research group that was established at the Pontifical John Paul II Institute for Studies on Marriage and Family in Rome in 1997. The Research Area wants to reflect on fundamental moral questions, seeking to interpret them in the light of Saint John Paul II's moral encyclical *Veritatis Splendor*. I am in numerous ways indebted to Rev. Livio Melina, who has served as the Institute's President for ten years until 2016 and who for many years has also been the Director of the Research Area, repeatedly inviting me to contribute to the Colloquia. This cooperation has continued also under the Research Area's new director since 2013, Rev. Juan José Pérez-Soba, to whom I would also like to express my appreciation.

Given that the first chapter reproduces my *lectio inauguralis*, the lecture formally opening my tenure as Professor on the Chair of Philosophical Anthropology at the Pontifical John Paul II Institute in Rome, I would like to convey my thankfulness to Professor Emeritus Stanisław Grygiel, my predecessor on that Chair, for his continued closeness, advice, and encouragement. A word of gratitude is also due, no doubt, to all my colleagues at the Institute for the always open and enriching exchange of ideas and opinions in the seminars of professors, in the different colloquia or in less formal settings like common lunches or dinners. I am thankful to all my students throughout the years, who with their questions and observations have been a precious source of inspiration. Also I am very grateful to Rev.

José Noriega, the Institute's editorial director, for his permission to republish texts that have previously come out in the Institute's scientific journal *Anthropotes*, or in the proceedings of the Institute's conferences. I would like to express my appreciation to Fabiana Ferrara, whose suggestion inspired the title of this work. Many thanks, finally, to Hansol Goo for proofreading the manuscript and to Rev. Tomás Vladymir Pérez Candelario, my assistant at the Institute, for his work on the bibliography and footnotes.

Stephan Kampowski
Spring 2017

PART ONE

Nature and Culture

Appreciating What Is Given

1

Dependence and Gratitude

What ultimately stills the fear of death is not hope or desire but remembrance and gratitude.

—HANNAH ARENDT, *LOVE AND SAINT AUGUSTINE*

The Human Condition:
Between Resentment and Gratitude

"NOW I AM BECOME Death, the destroyer of worlds."[1] These words, originally found in the sacred Hindu writing *Bhagavad Gita*, were uttered by Robert Oppenheimer when he witnessed the first successful test of an atomic bomb, the violence of which far exceeded the expectations of the scientists whom he directed and with whom he was working on the Manhattan Project, the purpose of which was to put Einstein's relativity theory to work in order to build a most deadly weapon and thus to bring World War II finally to a quick, though bloody and violent, end. For Hannah Arendt this day, July 16, 1945, marks nothing less than the end of modernity and the beginning of a new epoch.[2] With the advent of the atomic bomb, for the first time human beings have acquired the potential to extinguish all life on earth and possibly even to make the planet explode. Empires of the past

1. See Goodchild, *Robert Oppenheimer*, 162.
2. See Arendt, *Human Condition*, 6.

3

were known to rise and fall but the continuous succession of one kingdom by another was still thought to be lasting, with humanity itself being what guaranteed the existence of civilization. But now humanity itself is at risk to die off by the work of human hands. And the planet Earth, which, until that date, had been the quintessence of permanence in the shifty sand of human affairs, has now itself become as precarious as the human beings that inhabit it. We can thus say that July 16, 1945 ushered in a new liquid age, deprived as it were of the pillars of mundane permanence.

In this present context we are not proposing a historical reflection on the different epochs of human history. Rather, we want to consider the destructive tendency inherent in human ingenuity—the epitome of which is represented by the nuclear bomb, but which is, of course, also present in other human pursuits. Whence the destruction? What we want to propose here is that one of the roots of the human persons' destructive propensities is the difficulty to accept the fact that they are not the creators of themselves; humans are contingent and dependent beings. Life is given to us under certain conditions: for instance, we are born; we will have to die; we do not live alone in this world. Hannah Arendt refers to these givens of the human condition using the terms natality, mortality and human plurality.[3] These facts are an expression of our contingency, and for Arendt much of the technological revolution of the last centuries, of which the nuclear weapon is no doubt a legitimate child, can be seen as "a rebellion against human existence as it has been given."[4]

I do not wish to say that technology as such is evil. What I want to affirm is rather that there are certain destructive tendencies in technology, which derive—as I should like to propose—from the human beings' difficulty to be reconciled with their contingency. Ultimately, then, what I would like to reflect on is the meaning of the very fundamental fact that human beings are contingent and dependent. Taking my basic inspiration from Hannah Arendt, I would like to suggest that there are three ways in which we could respond to this fact: (1) confronted with our dependency we may resent this fact and seek to destroy all the conditions of our life that are not self-made, pretending complete self-sufficiency; (2) we may resign and despair at life's absurdity, which denies us self-sufficiency; 3) and

---

3. In total, Arendt lists six conditions of human existence: "life itself, natality and mortality, worldliness, plurality, and the earth" (ibid., 11).

4. Ibid., 2.

finally, we may be reconciled to the conditions under which life has been given to us, accept life as a gift and respond in gratitude.[5]

Human Contingency in Philosophical Reflection

As Alasdair MacIntyre points out, human dependency, as fundamental a fact as it is, has curiously been neglected or forgotten in philosophical reflections.[6] Thus he explains that Aristotle's reflections on ethics and politics center around the independent, healthy, strong, adult male citizen, while the experience of women, children, slaves, and workers is generally ignored.[7] In this way, these are essentially excluded from the good life. The ideal, in fact, is that of the magnanimous man, who "dislikes any recognition of his need for aid from and consolation by others."[8] In reality, however, the years in which human beings are relatively independent are rather few in number. In the old age people often become dependent on others once again as when young. A healthy adult becomes ill at times or may even become permanently disabled. Human beings are living organisms and are susceptible to aging, sickness, and death, and it would seem that a serious philosophical reflection should address these issues. Instead, much of the history of modern philosophy can be read as a single attempt to explain human existence without having to take recourse to our bodiliness. From René Descartes's *res cogitans* to Edmund Husserl's transcendental ego, the human being is not a body, or at least his

5. Arendt explicitly refers to the alternative between rebellion and gratitude in the "Concluding Remarks" of the first edition of her *Origins of Totalitarianism*, 438: "The first disastrous result of man's coming of age is that modern man has come to resent everything given, even his own existence—to resent the very fact that he is not the creator of the universe and himself. In this fundamental resentment, he refuses to see rhyme or reason in the given world. . . . The alternative to this resentment . . . would be a fundamental gratitude for the few elementary things that indeed are invariably given us, such as life itself, the existence of man and the world."

6. See MacIntyre, *Dependent Rational Animals*, 1: "From Plato to Moore and since there are usually, with some rare exceptions, only passing references to human vulnerability and affliction and to the connections between them and our dependence on others. Some of the facts of human limitation and of our consequent need of cooperation with others are generally acknowledged, but for the most part only then to be put on one side."

7. See ibid., 6: "In neither ethics nor politics did he [Aristotle] give any weight to the experience of those for whom the facts of affliction and dependence are most likely to be undeniable: women, slaves, and servants, those engaged in the productive labor of farmers, fishing crews, and manufacture."

8. Ibid., 7.

or her body can be "bracketed" (see Husserl's *epoché*). Great philosophers such as Immanuel Kant or David Hume seem to, at times, simply "forget the body"—to put it in Hans Jonas's terms.[9] The same holds true also for Martin Heidegger, for whom *Dasein* refers to a mortal, concerned existence, but is nonetheless curiously oblivious to the evident physical needs of a mortal being. Jonas comments on the issue: "Is the body ever mentioned? Is 'care' ever traced back to it, to concern about nourishment, for instance—indeed to *physical* needs at all? Except for its interior aspects, does Heidegger ever mention that side of our nature by means of which, quite externally, we ourselves belong to the world experienced by the senses, that world of which we, in blunt objective terms, are a part? Not that I know of."[10]

Forgetfulness of our body ultimately means forgetfulness of our contingent condition, of our vulnerability and dependency. And perhaps it is no accident that Heidegger, somewhat unmindful of the body, comes dangerously close to identifying *Dasein*, the one being for whom the question of being-as-such is an issue, with precisely this being-as-such, notwithstanding all his emphasis on the ontological difference.[11] But attempts to deny human contingency or, conversely spoken, the search for self-sufficiency, have existed in the philosophical tradition already since antiquity. The Stoics' ideals of *apatheia* (passionlessness) and *ataraxia* (undisturbedness) are nothing but expressions of the attempt at autarchy, thought to render the will all-powerful. If I always will what happens anyway, nothing can happen against my will,[12] even if I were to be roasted alive in Phalaris's bull.[13] Stoicism of course simply makes use of a mental trick,

9. See Jonas, *Phenomenon of Life*, 27–28.

10. Jonas, "Philosophy at the End of the Century," 820–21 (original emphasis).

11. See Arendt, "What Is Existential Philosophy?" 178–79: "Heidegger's philosophy makes man a kind of *summum ens*, a 'master of Being,' to the extent that existence and essence are identical in him. Once man was discovered to be the being he had for so long considered God to be, it then turned out that such a being is also, in fact, powerless and that there is consequently no 'master of Being.'"

12. Epictetus, *Enchiridion*, 4 (Paragraph VIII): "Seek not that the things which happen should happen as you wish; but wish the things which happen to be as they are, and you will have a tranquil flow of life."

13. See for example Seneca, "Letter 66 to Lucilius," 18: "I know what the reply to me might be at this point. 'Are you trying to persuade us of the proposition that it makes no difference whether someone experiences joy or lies upon the rack and wears of his torturer?' I could reply that Epicurus too says that the wise person, even if he is burned in the bull of Phalaris, will cry out, 'This is pleasant and it is nothing to me!'" There are important differences between Seneca and Epicurus. Here, however, Seneca seems to want to underline the commonalities.

quickly exposed by St. Augustine: If one cannot get what one wants, one simply wants what one can get.[14] But this could hardly be what it means to be all-powerful or self-sufficient.

Forgetfulness or straight-out denial of human contingency has, however, not been the only way in which our topic has been treated in the history of philosophy. Some thinkers have indeed thematized it as a problem. We may think for a moment of Emmanuel Levinas. Many of us may be familiar with what is perhaps his central idea: the first word that the face of the other tells me is, "Do not kill me!"[15] This actually sounds very good, and Levinas continues by speaking about one's infinite and absolute responsibility for the other, a responsibility that is not limited to simply not-doing-harm.[16] And yet, we must consider that every negation implies an affirmation, so that when Levinas claims that the first thing the face of the other tells me is, "Do not kill me," then he presumes that murder—and not responsibility—is the very first thing one thinks of when encountering the other. When I see my neighbor's Ferrari, it may tell me many things. "Do not steal me!" are its first words only if from the very beginning I am actually tempted to take it for myself.

But why would one be tempted to kill the other? For Levinas, the human being has a "totalizing" tendency, constantly tempted to reduce "the other" to "the same." This tendency finds particular expression in Western philosophy inasmuch as it presents itself as ontology.[17] In this context, freedom is understood as the self-sufficiency of reason, which, by its use of concepts, appropriates all things to itself, dominating them and depriving them of their alterity.[18] The other, Levinas says, "is the sole being I can wish to kill,"[19] and the reason for this is that only the other presents

14. Augustine, *On the Trinity*, XIII, 7, 10: "He wills, therefore, what he can, since he cannot have that which he wills."

15. See for example Levinas, *Totality and Infinity*, 199: "This infinity, stronger than murder, already resists us in his face, is his face, is the primordial *expression*, is the first word: 'you shall not commit murder'" (original emphasis).

16. See Levinas, *Ethics and Infinity*, 95–101.

17. See Levinas, *Totality and Infinity*, 43: "Western philosophy has most often been an ontology: a reduction of the other to the same. . . . The primacy of the same was Socrates's teaching: to receive nothing of the Other but what is in me, as though from all eternity I was in possession of what comes to me from the outside."

18. See ibid., 43–44: "The neutralization of the other who becomes a theme or an object . . . is precisely his reduction to the same. . . . To know amounts to grasping being out of nothing or reducing it to nothing, removing from it its alterity."

19. Ibid., 198.

me with true alterity, the other alone is a being I cannot absorb to myself; he or she is the one being that is out of my grasp.[20] The other in his or her otherness and transcendence is the constant reminder that I am not everything, that I am not self-sufficient, that I am limited. In other words, the other as other calls me into question, and to this calling into question Levinas gives the name "ethics."[21] There are indeed other subjects, other centers of significance in the world. Human plurality is a condition of my existence I need to come to terms with.

While for Hannah Arendt, human plurality is the cause of a "tremendous bliss,"[22] for Jean-Paul Sartre it rather has infernal repercussions: "Hell is other people,"[23] inasmuch as they reduce me to the ideas they have of me, constraining me to correspond to their expectations. Indeed, in existentialist philosophy the human being's difficulties in accepting his or her contingency find an exemplary expression. For the existentialist pathos, "existence precedes essence."[24] There is nothing given that defines my essence; in my existential choices I decide who and what I want to be. There is no external criterion to guide, no horizon of significance to encompass me. "We are left alone," Jean-Paul Sartre writes, "and without excuse. That is what I mean when I say that man is condemned to be free: condemned, because he did not create himself, yet nevertheless free, because once cast into the world, he is responsible for everything he does."[25] But why am I "*condemned* to be free"? I was never asked to exist. There is a givenness and a facticity about my being born, which has to be dealt with and which would seem to go against the existentialist grain. Thus, Sartre is forced to

20. See ibid.: "Murder exercises a power over what escapes power. It is still a power, for the face expresses itself in the sensible, but already impotency, because the face rends the sensible. The alterity that is expressed in the face provides the unique 'matter' possible for total negation. I can wish to kill only an existent absolutely independent, which exceeds my powers infinitely, and therefore does not oppose them but paralyzes the very power of power. The Other is the sole being I can wish to kill."

21. See ibid., 43: "A calling into question of the same—which cannot occur within the egoistic spontaneity of the same—is brought about by the other. We name this calling into question of my spontaneity by the presence of the Other ethics."

22. Arendt, "Concluding Remarks," 438–39: "We can reconcile ourselves to the variety of mankind, to the differences between human beings . . . only through insight into the tremendous bliss that man was created with the power of procreation, that not a single man but Men inhabit the earth."

23. Sartre, "No Exit," 45.

24. Sartre, *Existentialism Is a Humanism*, 22.

25. Ibid., 29

8

raise himself this objection: "Someone will say, 'I did not ask to be born.'"[26] He is not particularly sympathetic to this affirmation, calling it "a naïve way of throwing greater emphasis on our facticity."[27] He then continues by arguing that despite the fact that I did not actually and literally choose to be born, I am nonetheless responsible for everything, "except for my very responsibility," for, as he admits, "I am not the foundation of my being."[28] He then seeks to find a way in which he could say that "I *choose* being born," namely in the sense that "I am ashamed of being born or I am astonished at it or I rejoice over it, or in attempting to get rid of my life, I affirm that I live and I assume this life as bad."[29] For him it is due to the various attitudes that I can assume towards my birth that "I can not ask '*Why* was I born?' or curse the day of my birth or declare that I did not ask to be born." These attitudes "are absolutely nothing else but ways of assuming this birth in full responsibility and making it *mine*."[30]

But in the end, this somewhat cumbersome argument only reveals the problem in its full force. As much as I can take a stance towards the fact that I was born, the issue remains: I did not choose it, and indeed, it is something I could not possibly have chosen. My natality—to use Hannah Arendt's term—necessarily precedes every choice of mine, given that only existing beings can choose. Nor was I asked whether I wanted to exist, which is impossible for the same reason: only existing beings can be asked anything.

The question of coming to terms with one's birth is also at the center of Albert Camus's philosophy, inasmuch as he claims that the biggest question of philosophy is nothing other than the problem of suicide.[31] Suicide, when it is committed with freedom and premeditation, is not one way among others of dealing with the human condition of *mortality*. Rather it is an implicit or explicit rebellion against one's condition of *natality*, "the refusal to take the oath of loyalty to life,"[32] as G. K. Chesterton formulates it. It is the supremely destructive act. For Chesterton, "the man who kills a man, kills a man. The man who kills himself, kills all men; as far as he is concerned he wipes out

---

26. Sartre, *Being and Nothingness*, 710.

27. Ibid.

28. Ibid.

29. Ibid. (original emphasis).

30. Ibid. (original emphasis).

31. Camus, *Myth of Sisyphus*, 3: "There is but one truly serious philosophical problem, and that is suicide."

32. Chesterton, *Orthodoxy*, 78.

the world."[33] Persons who kill themselves—freely and deliberately—refuse all the goods of the world, not allowing any of these to provide them with reasons for living. Thus they offend all of them,[34] affirming their supremacy over all things by calling all things unworthy of them.

The Human Person Confronted with Birth

Our present topic is dependence and gratitude. So far we have looked at dependence and the creaturely contingency it implies: we are born, we will have to die, there are other persons inhabiting the world with us. Of these three conditions, what perhaps reminds us most of our dependency, what most contradicts any striving towards self-sufficiency, is the fact of our birth. It is most completely and by strict logical necessity out of the reach of our will. Our birth is nothing we could have chosen, and it is in the past. Though the Tradition has defined human beings as mortals, Hannah Arendt seems well justified in proposing that they may also be defined as "natals."[35] For the human person who is looking for self-sufficiency, the fact of our birth may well be a greater scandal than our death. In death, there is no logical contradiction in the thought of an earthly or heavenly immortality, and in fact, many religious faiths speak of the latter while a good number of scientists strive to achieve the former. In contrast, the fact that we are born, that our life had a beginning, cannot be changed, or abolished or in any way remedied, not even in thought. It is a strict, logical necessity. Thus, as we continue to discuss creaturely dependence and contingency in its relation to gratitude we shall mostly speak of it in terms of our birth or natality. So far we have seen *that* it is difficult to come to terms with our contingency. In what follows, we will try to explain *why* this is the case and *how* our contingency could actually lead us to a sense of gratitude instead of the sense of resentment we have seen thus far.

33. Ibid.

34. See ibid.: "His act is worse (symbolically considered) than any rape or dynamite outrage. For it destroys all buildings: it insults all women. The thief is satisfied with diamonds; but the suicide is not: that is his crime. He cannot be bribed, even by the blazing stones of the Celestial City. The thief compliments the things he steals, if not the owner of them. But the suicide insults everything on earth by not stealing it. He defiles every flower by refusing to live for its sake. There is not a tiny creature in the cosmos at whom his death is not a sneer."

35. See Arendt, "Willing," in *Life of the Mind,* 109.

Why is it so difficult for us to be reconciled with our birth? Where is the root of the impossible human striving for self-sufficiency, with its resentful and destructive effects? A being that is born does not have in itself the reasons for being. It has an origin; it is contingent; it is but it could also not be. Hence, *prima facie* its existence is precarious. It remains dependent on its origin. It would seem that to *be* fully, this being would have to emancipate itself from its origin. As Angelo Cardinal Scola points out, it seems that here we find one of the roots of the "eclipse of fatherhood" in existentialist thought and in the modern mentality in general.[36] Only independent existence would seem to be fully assured existence, while dependence is tantamount to fear, the fear of losing oneself.[37] Thus fear is the driving force behind human striving for self-sufficiency, emancipation, or independence. My birth, and the past in general, reminds me of my contingency. As Nietzsche puts it, the will cannot will backwards.[38] The will has no power over the past to change it; and if there is to be a meaning, if there is supposed to be any solution to the human person's fearful predicament, it has to be in the future. It is here, in the future, that one will have to seek the meaning of one's existence, since only the future is—to some extent—under the influence of one's will. Only the future falls within the range of one's power to build and to create—after having first destroyed everything that was not made by oneself. Human beings who cannot find their origin, the meaning of their existence, in their past, in the gift of their Creator, will need to look to the future that they construct themselves. This is the meaning of Hannah Arendt's profound insight: "The moment man defines himself no longer as *creatura Dei*, he will find it very difficult not to think of himself, consciously or unconsciously, as *homo faber*."[39]

36. See Scola, *Nuptial Mystery*, 239–43.

37. See Arendt, *Love and Saint Augustine,* 11: "Life on earth is a living death, *mors vitalis,* or *vita mortalis*. It is altogether determined by death; indeed it is more properly called death. For the constant fear that rules it prevents living, unless one equates being alive with being afraid. This basic fear guides all our fears of specific evils. By putting an end to life, death is at the same time the cause of the constant worry of life about itself—the endless concern about its transient happiness—and about life after death."

38. Nietzsche, *Thus Spoke Zarathustra*, 121: "'It was': that is the will's gnashing of teeth and loneliest sorrow. Powerless with respect to what has been done—it is an angry spectator of all that is past. Backwards the will is unable to will; that it cannot break time and time's desire—that is the will's loneliest sorrow. . . . Thus did the will, the liberator, take to hurting: and upon all that can suffer it takes revenge for its inability to go backwards. This, yes this alone, is what *revenge* itself is: the will's ill-will toward time and its 'It was'" (original emphasis).

39. Arendt, "Eggs Speak Up," 283.

From the perspective of a precarious existence looking for safety in what it builds itself, the justification for my being cannot come from the past, which only serves to remind me of my endangered condition. As *homo faber* I cannot *find* my purpose but have to *create* it. There is no activity meaningful in itself; nothing is done for its own sake. Rather, everything I do has to be justified by its future use. *Homo faber*, the maker of products, justifies all he or she does by reference to the use it has for future products, while the justification of these in turn lies in the use they have for yet other future products. However, the question of what is the use of use inevitably remains unanswered.[40] When human beings are not rooted in their origin in the Creator, they will take their bearings from the future that they themselves create. In their rebellion against everything that is given, human persons as *homo faber* would seem to aim at one ultimate goal, which is to create themselves anew, to create a new humanity that does not owe its existence to any cause that is not the human being him- or herself. This new, self-made human being would finally be independent and self-sufficient, so that the scandal of birth may be averted.

Hans Jonas rightly points out how little the fabricators and designers of the new human being appreciate what has been given.[41] The fears of unknown dangers involved in genetically manipulating crops lead people to protest on the streets, but how much greater are the risks involved in manipulating human nature? What is going on in the minds of scientists who are creating human-animal chimeras, justifying their research with the hope of one day being able to grow human organs from a pig?[42] Undoubtedly, Berthold Brecht is right when he says that no one escaping from a burning house will ask whether it is raining outside.[43] In the face of ultimate dangers, we may have to be willing at times to take ultimate risks. But if human nature were indeed so contemptible as to justify any risk for

40. See Arendt, *Human Condition*, 154: "The ideal of usefulness itself, like the ideals of other societies, can no longer be conceived as something needed in order to have something else; it simply defies questioning about its own use. Obviously there is no answer to the question which Lessing once put to the utilitarian philosophers of his time: 'And what is the use of use?' The perplexity of utilitarianism is that it gets caught in the unending chain of means and ends without ever arriving at some principle which could justify the category of means and end, that is, of utility itself."

41. See Jonas, *Imperative of Responsibility*, 34. For a more detailed analysis of Hans Jonas's critique of the utopian tendencies inherent to modern science and technology, see Kampowski, *Greater Freedom*, 65–127.

42. See Regalado, "Human-Animal Chimeras."

43. See Brecht, "Buddha's Parable," 290–92.

improving it, then the scientists themselves, who are also human, could not possibly attribute to themselves the wisdom to know how to make it better. Then they themselves are from a corrupt stock, and as such not qualified to create the new and better human being.[44] As a guiding principle for our technological age, Hans Jonas proposes this: to appreciate what has been given to us and to leave untouched the image of the human person made in the image of God.[45] We must not make for ourselves an image of the human being, any more than we must make for ourselves an image of God.

For this, of course, we will have to be reconciled with our natality and indeed with all the conditions under which life has been given to us. To appreciate who and what we are means to speak of gratitude for what has been given, a gratitude that is the alternative of resentment. Those who are resentful know that they have received something and precisely resent this fact, inasmuch as it reminds them of their dependence. Hence they refuse to remember, since remembrance is of the past, which cannot be changed; it is outside their power and thus potentially dangerous. They resent their birth, their death, and the fact of human plurality: they have not made themselves, they are not immortal, and they are not alone and hence neither all-powerful nor completely sovereign. Their deepest desire is to "remedy" these conditions, a desire which for Hannah Arendt is the root of totalitarianism.[46] Those who are grateful, in contrast, receive the basic conditions under which life has been given to them as a gift.[47] But why is this so difficult?

We may think here of Jesus's parable of the two debtors (Matt 18:23–35). One plausible explanation of the puzzling behavior of the one to whom the king had forgiven an enormous debt and who was quite unwilling to forgive the petty sum of his fellow-servant is that the wicked servant had never really accepted the king's gift, that he was not happy or grateful about being forgiven but inwardly planned on paying back the whole sum as soon

44. See Jonas, *Imperative of Responsibility*, 32–33.

45. See Jonas, "Contemporary Problems in Ethics," 181: "We simply must not try to fixate man in any image of our own definition and thereby cut off the as yet unrevealed promises of the image of God."

46. See Arendt, *Origins of Totalitarianism*, 456: "It is in the very nature of totalitarian regimes to demand unlimited power. Such power can only be secured if literally all men, without a single exception, are reliably dominated in every aspect of their life."

47. For a discussion of the gift as anthropological, philosophical and theological concept, see Mauss, *The Gift*; Godbout and Caillé, *World of the Gift*; Derrida, *Given Time*; Marion, *Being Given*; López, *Gift and the Unity of Being*; Kupczak, *Gift and Communion*.

as he was able, attempting to gather money from wherever he could. Indeed, quite plausibly for a virtuous pagan the fact of having been forgiven such an enormous sum would have been tantamount to a grave humiliation. For the ancients, virtuous persons were magnanimous: they knew how and where to spend the right amount, but they did not know how to receive. They remembered what they had given but were too embarrassed to think about what they had received,[48] as receiving implies the acknowledgement of dependence. Furthermore, the logic of giving and receiving goes beyond the objects or services exchanged; it objectively establishes a relationship between the two parties. The giver is present in the gift. In accepting the gift, the receiver accepts the giver. As Kenneth Schmitz affirms: "The thing given, then, is not simply a detachable item, an independent thing in its own right; nor is it to be understood as an external substitute for the giver. It is a *token* of him, that is, it is not only *his*: it is *he*."[49] Hence for both parties the logic of giving and receiving involves transcendence—and a risk to their autarchy. In Jesus's parable the king is evidently angry at his servant: "Should not you have had mercy on your fellow servant, as I had mercy on you?" (Matt 18:33). But was he rightly upset? Was it not an issue just between the two servants? No, it was also a matter between the first servant and the king. By his behavior, the servant showed that he did not receive the gift and that he wanted to pay the money back. In this way, he also rejected the giver, the king.

Human existence is precarious existence, and inasmuch as it is precarious, it is fearful. And fear may well be the driving force of much if not most of the destruction caused by human hands. But there is a way of responding to the conditions under which my life has been given to me other than seeking to destroy them. I could trust. I could trust that my origin, in which the reasons for my being are contained, is good and reliable, that he will not later ask me for the debt from which he had previously claimed to have released me. The question of the origin then assumes central importance. Is it safe to trust it? If the human beings' origin were in a random chance event, or in the arbitrary sports of a demiurge, it would be understandable for them to seek to emancipate themselves from their source and to find

48. See Aristotle, *Nicomachean Ethics*, IV, 3, 1124b10–15: "[The great-souled man] is fond of conferring benefits, but ashamed to receive them, because the former is a mark of superiority and the latter of inferiority. . . . The great-souled are thought to have a good memory for any benefit they have conferred, but a bad memory for those which they have received (since the recipient of a benefit is the inferior of his benefactor, whereas they desire to be superior."

49. Schmitz, *The Gift*, 59 (original emphases).

objection at the impossibility of ever completely doing so. Birth would then indeed be a scandal. If, on the contrary, the human origin were to be in an omnipotent and omnibenevolent God, who created the world out of love, then human existence could be assured, even if it is dependent. Dependence would not have to be a reason for fear. It could be trustingly affirmed. By the very constitution of their existence, human beings are believers.[50] Given that they are beings that are born, they have to believe something about their origin. Human persons necessarily ask themselves the *magna quaestio*, the great question: "Where do I come from and where am I going to?"[51] What they believe about their origin will make all the difference for their lives. The answer they give to this question will decide whether or not they will be able to be reconciled to their natality, capable of entrusting themselves to their origin, which is also their end. As Blondel puts it: "It is true, the option is imposed on us . . . It is the total determinism of human life that hangs from this supreme alternative: either exclude from ourselves any other will than our own, or hand ourselves over to the being that we are not as the only salutary one. Man aspires to be a god: to be god without God and against God, to be god through God and with God, that is the dilemma."[52] Ultimately, this alternative will decide whether human beings will respond to their contingency with resentment or rather with gratitude, which is the true sense of an existence gratuitously received as a gift.

Do I and can I believe that God exists and that he is good? If I cannot, then I will have to fear for my life, I will have to aspire to self-sufficiency and independence, emancipating myself from my source, whatever it may be. The Tradition calls the human striving for independence by the name

50. In his masterpiece *Action*, Maurice Blondel draws attention to this fact, reflecting on the infinite horizon of human action. According to him, in my every act I do not only seek the immediate object of my will, but at the same time something that is completely incommensurable with it, something that infinitely surpasses everything I could imagine or grasp: I desire something infinite, which is why the idea of God imposes itself on me: "Because I am forced to conceive and to assign a higher term to my thought and my action, it is also necessary for me to feel the need to equal my thought and my life to it. The idea of God . . . is the inevitable complement of human action" (*Action*, 326). Considering Blondel's thought completely valid, here we would simply like to affirm that human beings are constitutively believers inasmuch as they are confronted with the fact of their natality, they need to believe something about their origin, which by definition is something that transcends them, independently from how it is called: God, chance, necessity, or another name.

51. For a rich reflection on the *magna quaestio* and an attempt at giving a response in terms of an anthropology of communion, see Grygiel, *Extra comunionem personarum*.

52. Blondel, *Action*, 328.

of sin,[53] precisely because by seeking its independence the contingent being takes a negative stance towards God. It implicitly says to its Creator, "You are not to be trusted. You are not good. Your plans for me are deceitful." This seems to be the core of the account of the first sin committed by human beings as told by the book of Genesis. The serpent acts as a master of suspicion, sowing doubts about the goodness of God, suggesting he could be the author of a truly ridiculous commandment: "Did God say, 'You shall not eat of any tree of the garden?'" (Gen 3:1). The tempter then proceeds by suggesting that God was afraid of Adam and Eve, fearing them as potential rivals and trying to suppress them: "God knows that when you eat of it your eyes will be opened, and you will be like God" (Gen 3:5). After having suggested that God cannot be trusted and that his plans are not good, the serpent continues suggesting that it may be safer for them to trust only in themselves: You will know "good and evil" (Gen 3:5). What could be more important to know than that? Knowing good and evil, the tempter proposes, will make you independent of a God whose intentions for you are at best doubtful. He is afraid of you and you should be afraid of him. Do not trust him, but dare to know for yourselves. Independence is the ideal and fear is the driving force. Here is the foundation of evil, strife, and resentment: my existence is threatened, precarious, and poor. To be free I need to be independent and do away with everything that threatens my self-sufficiency. Dependence, in contrast, is tolerable only on one condition: if it is safe to trust the one on whom I depend.

Remembering the Gift

But how do I know that it is safe to trust my origin? How do I know that my life is really a gift and my birth not a scandal? Here it seems that any theoretical reflection comes to the end of its road. There are strong philosophical arguments for God's existence, and yet few people become believers simply by reading St. Thomas's five ways. Philosophy can also point out quite cogently with Søren Kierkegaard that God's goodness follows necessarily from

53. See for example John Paul II, *Veritatis Splendor*, no. 102: "What is the ultimate source of this inner division of man? His history of sin begins when he no longer acknowledges the Lord as his Creator and himself wishes to be the one who determines, with complete independence, what is good and what is evil." For independence as sin, see also the way in which Hannah Arendt sums up St. Augustine's thought: "What becomes sinful here is independence as such." "The world's sinfulness derives from its origin independent of God" (*Love and Saint Augustine*, 87, 103).

his omnipotence:[54] and yet this argument just by itself will do little to induce trust. The essence of Christianity, Pope Benedict XVI emphasizes, does not consist in a doctrine—though of course it does have doctrines—but in an event: the event of the encounter with the person of Christ.[55] And the first thing that this encounter tells me is this: "You are loved." Here lies the importance of Benedict's words: "*We have come to believe in God's love*: in these words the Christian can express the fundamental decision of his life."[56] If I know that I am loved, I can trust. If I can trust, I can receive the gift along with the giver and renounce my pretense of self-sufficiency. If I can renounce my pretense of self-sufficiency, I can be grateful for what I have received. And this gratitude in turn will inspire within me a sense of generosity, which will henceforth inform all my actions and all my life.

At the beginning of the Christian way, there is a contingent event, which consists in a call by the one who has loved me, who has created and redeemed me. The response to this call is made possible by grace and takes on the form of a conversion.[57] Yet I cannot give this conversion to myself. To paraphrase the interpretation Hannah Arendt gives of St. Augustine, the return to his or her origin is not in the power of the created being. Rather, for this conversion, the creature depends on the Creator.[58] We are ultimately dependent on God even for being able to acknowledge our dependence. For Arendt, if the human person "could be said to have an essential nature at all, it would be lack of self-sufficiency."[59] But we are not even sufficient to

54. See Kierkegaard, *Papers and Journals,* 234 (46 VII I A 181): "That is why one human being cannot make another wholly free, because the one with the power is himself captive in his possession of it and is therefore continually coming into a false relationship with the one he wants to make free. . . . Only omnipotence can revoke itself while giving, and it is just this circumstance that forms the recipient's independence. God's omnipotence is therefore his goodness. For goodness is to give oneself completely but in such a way that by omnipotently retracting oneself one makes the recipient independent."

55. See Benedict XVI, *Deus Caritas Est,* no. 1: "Being Christian is not the result of an ethical choice or a lofty idea, but the encounter with an event, a person, which gives life a new horizon and a decisive direction."

56. Ibid. (original emphasis).

57. See Melina, *Epiphany of Love,* 96: "Since the divine call always surprises us in a condition of sin, the positive response, which is possible through grace, takes the form of a conversion. In it, freedom fully grasps the initial gift and, by means of it, dynamically unites human actions."

58. See Arendt, *Love and Saint Augustine,* 87: "Its lack of power makes the creature depend on the Creator once again and more decisively. It is up to God whether man who has already set out on the world, will ever reach this self-demanded goal."

59. Ibid., 19.

ourselves to acknowledge this fact and be reconciled to it. Is there anything we can do, or are we condemned to quietism? Love is indeed the first gift, which enables us to receive every other gift.[60] If there is a problem, it does not lie with God, who certainly wants to give it. The problem lies with our capacity to receive, and even this capacity to receive will have to be called a gift. Yet here seems to be indeed at least one thing that we can do: we can attempt to dispose ourselves to receiving the gift, and one of the ways of doing so would seem to be remembrance.

The psalmist's exhortation "Remember the wonderful works that he has done" (Ps 105:5) may still manifest itself to be a fundamental moral exhortation for a temporal being that has its existence between past and future. Remembering our birth, for instance, indeed confronts us with our contingency. It is something that has been given gratuitously. How remembering the gratuitous nature of one's existence can influence one's entire attitude towards life and death and thus have clear moral implications, is expressed beautifully in a letter Arendt wrote to Mary McCarthy on the occasion of the death of a common friend. Previously MaCarthy's partner had referred to his death as "hateful." Arendt responds in this way:

> Mary, look, I think I know how sad you are and how serious this loss is. . . . Still—if you just say "hateful" you will have to say hateful to many more things if you want to be consistent. One could look upon one's whole life as a being-given *and* being-taken away; that starts already with life itself, given at birth, taken away with death; and the whole time in-between could easily be looked at as standing under the same law. . . .
>
> I looked up once more the Jewish death prayers: they, that is, the *kaddish*, are a single praise of God, the name of the dead one is not even mentioned: The underlying notion is what is inscribed on all Jewish funeral homes: The Lord hath given, the Lord hath taken away, blessed be the Lord. Or: Don't complain if something is taken away that was given you but which you did not necessarily *own*. And don't forget, to be taken away, it had first to be given. If you believed you owned, if you forgot that it was given, that is just too bad for you.[61]

Remembering that life was *given* in the first place implies acknowledging that we do not own it. It did not have to be and it did not have to be

---

60. See Aquinas, *Summa Theologica*, I, 38, 2: "Love has the nature of a first gift, through which all free gifts are given."

61. Arendt and McCarthy, *Between Friends*, 307 (original emphases).

this way. Remembering birth, we can look our contingency in the eye. But it is not only a question of remembering the *fact* that life was given, but also of remembering its goodness. Then remembrance can indeed lead to gratitude. We easily tend to forget. For anything to be taken, it first had to be given. For there to be any evil, there first has to be some good of which it is a privation. And, as St. Augustine points out, even those who claim that their life is so miserable that they would prefer not to exist make these claims on the firm ground of being. Thus they are not to be believed in what they say. In their heart of hearts, what they truly seek is not non-being, which for Augustine could never be the object of a choice, but rather rest.[62] Indeed, for the Bishop of Hippo the desire to escape from unhappiness speaks to us of the love for the being that we have already received and for which we can be grateful: "Therefore, if you want to avoid unhappiness, love the will to exist which is in you. If, more and more, you desire to be, you will approach that which is in the highest degree. Give thanks, now, that you are."[63]

"A Christian," Joseph Ratzinger writes, "is someone who knows that apart from all this he lives first and foremost as the beneficiary of a bounty."[64] But in some sense this is true of every human being; it is an anthropological affirmation. It is a fact that we need to remember. We need to open ourselves to the primary evidence of the goodness of life and all the goods that come along with it. Life with all its goods has come to us gratuitously. To say it with Livio Melina: "In effect, the being of creation itself, and therefore of human existence as well, is not a pure *datum*, a given, but a *donum*, a gift. It derives from a freedom and is directed toward a freedom; that is, it is situated within the dynamics of an interpersonal dialogue. 'Gift' is the original name of created being."[65] We need to make attempts to remember its gratuitousness and its goodness.

62. Augustine, *On Free Choice of the Will*, III, 8: "See how foolish and inconsistent it is to say: 'I would prefer not to be, than to be unhappy.' The man who says, 'I prefer this to that,' chooses something: but 'not to be' is not something, but nothing. Therefore, you cannot in any way choose rightly when you choose something that does not exist. . . . When someone who believes that at his death he will cease to exist is driven by unendurable troubles to yearn for death, he makes his decision and takes his life. He has the false opinion that he will be totally annihilated, but his natural feeling is a longing for peace. What is at peace, however, is not nothing: on the contrary, it exists to a greater degree than something that is not at peace. . . . Therefore, just as no one can will in any way not to exist, so no one who exists should be ungrateful for the goodness of the Creator."

63. Ibid., III, 7.

64. Ratzinger, *Introduction to Christianity*, 196.

65. Melina, *Building a Culture*, 16.

But what are we to say of those who are handicapped, disabled, in utter pain, living life in misery? How would their life be a gift to them? The first thing to respond to this is that the difference between the so-called disabled and the so-called healthy is not one of quality but one of degree. For all of us, it is a question of being more or less dependent on others. At some points in our lives—particularly in childhood, old age, and during illness—we all experience some kind of dependence. Very often it is not the more-disabled who find their existence so intolerable. Their existence is disturbing rather for the less-disabled, for whom the existence of the more-disabled is a reminder of their own precariousness. We need to remember the goodness of life. God is the lover of the living, as Scripture tells us (see Wis 11:26). He hates none of the things that he has made (see Wis 11:24). It is particularly the disabled, the disfigured, the suffering that speak to us of the unconditional value of human life that is precious already for the simple fact that it *is*, regardless of everything else. They remind us, in other words, of the primacy of being over having of which the Second Vatican Council speaks,[66] basing itself on a conceptual distinction elaborated by Gabriel Marcel.[67] We have to remember birth, remember the goodness of the gift of life that we have received.

Birth, as the manifestation of our life to the world, reminds us that our life is a being-from. Life, Benedict XVI says, is relationship.[68] The fullness of life is in communion. To this everyone is invited, also those who are in some ways disabled. Life means communion and communion means communication. Now in this communication not everyone gives or receives the same things. But even of the most disabled and dependent persons it is not true that they only receive and give nothing. As Robert Spaemann points out, very often these give much more than they receive. What they give is that they bring out the best in others,[69] which is why the way a society treats those who are more dependent is a test for its humanity.

---

66. Second Vatican Council, *Gaudium et Spes*, no. 35: "People are of greater value for what they are than for what they have."

67. See Marcel, *Being and Having*.

68. Benedict XVI, *Spe Salvi*, no. 27: "Life in its true sense is not something we have exclusively in or from ourselves: it is a relationship."

69. See Spaemann, *Persons*, 244: "Friendship and erotic love develop mainly in response to the beloved's individual personal properties. A disabled person may lack such properties, and it is by lacking them that they constitute the paradigm for a human community of recognizing *selves*, rather than simply valuing useful or attractive *properties*. They evoke the best in human beings; they evoke the true ground of human self-respect" (original emphases).

The Principle of All Things: Eternal Reason and Eternal Love

Human beings are "natals." They are contingent and receive their being from another. What or who that other is makes all the difference for their lives. If they cannot trust their origin, they will naturally be afraid and seek to emancipate themselves from it by striving for self-sufficiency. They will find meaning and security only in the things they have made themselves and mistrust anything given, seeking to destroy it and replace it by the works of their own hands. They will not like to remember but look to the future as a harbor of possible safety. If, on the other hand, their source is love, if the eternal *logos* or principle of all things is *agape*,[70] then they can trust. Their existence will be assured. They can have confidence and do not need to be afraid. They can remember and will want to remember. They will consider their lives as a free gift for which to respond in gratitude.

As Ratzinger points out, we are confronted here with what he calls a "basic choice."[71] If the origin of all things is found in chance and necessity,[72] in whatever is neither reason nor love, then we live in the absurd, and we will need to be afraid. There is, however, not a single philosophical argument in favor of this latter position. Whatever its motivation may be, it cannot be the result of a philosophical reflection, because philosophy, inasmuch as it is a rational discourse, presupposes the intelligibility of the world, which is negated by the position that claims that the origin of all that is, is in the irrational. If however the principle of all things is Eternal Reason and Eternal Love, then we are dealing here with a Being to which we can entrust ourselves and which ensures that our lives have a meaning from their very

70. See Ratzinger, "In Search of Peace," 97: "God is Logos. But there is a second characteristic. . . . Precisely because he is sovereign, because he is the Creator, because he embraces everything, he is Relation and he is Love. Faith in the Incarnation of God in Jesus Christ, and in his suffering and death for mankind, is the supreme expression of a conviction that the heart of all morality, the heart of being itself and its deepest principle, is love."

71. See Ratzinger, "Truth of Christianity?" 181: "The question is whether reason, or rationality, stands at the beginning of all things and is grounded in the basis of all things or not. The question is whether reality originated on the basis of chance and necessity . . . and thus, from what is irrational, that is, whether reason, being a chance by-product of irrationality and floating in an ocean of irrationality, is ultimately just as meaningless; or whether the principle that represents the fundamental conviction of Christian faith and of its philosophy remains true: 'In principio erat Verbum'—at the beginning of all things stands the creative power of reason."

72. See Monod, *Chance and Necessity*.

beginning: we can have trust. But here, too, philosophy cannot help us with an independent judgment. Every philosophical discourse, at least inasmuch as it claims to propose arguments and make judgments, has already made its choice in favor of the second option, presupposing the world's intelligibility. I cannot, without begging the question, give rational arguments to someone who negates the validity of rational arguments. Whoever gives reasons presupposes that reasons exist and count. All this can only be the case if we are not living in the absurd. And we do not live in the absurd only if we do not come from the absurd (chance and necessity) but from Reason, a Reason that then has also revealed himself to be Love.

In this context it is useful to look at how Robert Spaemann discusses the objection that Friedrich Nietzsche raises against the traditional proofs for God's existence. Nietzsche claims that in the end they presuppose what they want to demonstrate. Inasmuch as they are cosmological proofs, starting from our experience of the world, they presuppose the intelligibility of the world, which can only be affirmed under the condition that we also affirm the existence of God as its eternal, rational origin: "The classical proofs for the existence of God sought to demonstrate that the claim that God exists is a true one. They presupposed that there is such a thing as truth, and that the world possesses intelligible structures that are accessible to the mind. These structures have their ground, to be sure, in the world's divine origin, but they are nevertheless immediately accessible to us and for that reason are able to lead us to this ground."[73] On one point Nietzsche would probably find himself in agreement with Spaemann and Ratzinger: for the world to be intelligible, open to being known by human reason, for there to be reason and truth, it is necessary that God exists. Proclaiming the "death of God," Nietzsche in fact intended to negate all this: reason, truth, meaning. Rather, he wanted to affirm life even in the midst of the absurd. Thus, Spaemann continues: "Nietzsche wrote 'that we too, we enlightened ones, we free spirits of the nineteenth century, we still draw our fire from Christian belief, which was also Plato's belief, that God is truth and that the truth is divine.' But for Nietzsche, precisely this notion is a self-deception. There is no truth; there are only idiosyncrasies, which may be either useful or harmful."[74] Seeing all that falls together with God's existence, Spaemann arrives at the opposite option: "If the experience of the world as the open space of a self-manifesting reality can only be had at the price of the af-

73. See Spaemann, "Undying Rumor," 189–90.

74. Ibid., 190.

firmation of God's existence, then for those who would like to continue thinking of themselves as free beings capable of truth, this will be the most convincing argument for God's existence."[75]

Thus, philosophy cannot release us from our choice in favor or against the intelligibility and the goodness of our origin, as if it were a neutral court of appeal. It is not neutral in this respect. What makes a difference in the end is not an idea or argument, but an event: the encounter with the love of God in the person of Christ.[76] This no one can give to him- or herself. But we can prepare ourselves for it, precisely by remembering our birth, the gratuitousness of our existence and its goodness. Opening our eyes for the gift, we may well be able to receive and to accept the gift along with the Giver. In this way we can predispose ourselves to the event of an encounter that allows us to live our life from a sense of gratitude. What philosophy, inasmuch as it is rational discourse, can finally tell us here is that it is reasonable to believe in the creative Reason, opening ourselves to the one who has said of himself "I am . . . the life" (John 14:6).

---

75. Spaemann, "Gottesbeweise nach Nietzsche," 53 (my own translation).
76. Benedict XVI, *Deus Caritas Est*, no. 1.

2

Judgment and Common Sense

Reverence not thy neighbor in his fall:

And refrain not to speak in the time of salvation.

—SIR 4:27–28, DOUAY-RHEIMS

Scripture on Judgment

A Contradiction?

"LINGUISTIC INVESTIGATIONS HAVE SHOWN that NT allusions to judging and judgment are mostly connected with God's eschatological judgment of mankind. Justice and righteousness emanate from God and Christ. For this reason human beings are explicitly forbidden to pass judgment on their fellow men."[1] After reading these observations by Elisabeth Schüssler-Fiorenza, we will immediately be able to think of many well-known passages from Scripture that can be cited in support. There are Jesus's own authoritative words in the Sermon on the Mount: "Judge not, that you be not judged" (Matt 7:1). In his Letter to the Romans, St. Paul strongly exhorts the Jewish and Gentile Christians not to judge each other: "Therefore, you have no excuse, O man, whoever you are, when you judge another; for in passing judgment upon him you condemn yourself" (Rom

---

1. Schüssler-Fiorenza, "Judging and Judgment," 4.

2:1), and the Epistle of James explicitly seems to want to leave the judgment up to God, just the way Schüssler-Fiorenza claims: "There is one lawgiver and judge, he who is able to save and to destroy. But who are you that you judge your neighbor?" (Jas 4:12). It is before God's throne of judgment that each of us stands. Who are we to pass judgment on the servant of another, whose "Master is able to make him stand" (Rom 14:4)?

But then again, Schüssler-Fiorenza's claims notwithstanding, in the New Testament we find many verses that seem to take a different stance on judgment. On numerous occasions, St. Paul himself does not hesitate to express a quick and acute judgment on others. "God shall strike you, you whitewashed wall!" (Acts 23:3), he says to a judge who treats him unjustly: "Are you sitting to judge me according to the law, and yet contrary to the law you order me to be struck?" (Acts 23:3). It is true that Paul apologizes, but only upon learning that the addressee of his words was the Jewish high priest in person—and after all it is written, "You shall not speak evil of a ruler of your people" (Acts 23:5). Another, perhaps even more remarkable instance of St. Paul's judgment, is the episode in Antioch where the apostle of the Gentiles thinks it is necessary to reprimand publically no one other than the rock of Peter himself, who had fallen into hypocritical behavior: "If you, though a Jew, live like a Gentile and not like a Jew, how can you compel the Gentiles to live like Jews?" (Gal 2:14). There are, of course, more passages: In First Corinthians, St. Paul rebukes the community for tolerating an open sinner in their midst, exhorting them "not to associate with anyone who bears the name of brother if he is guilty of immorality or greed, or is an idolater, reviler, drunkard, or robber—not even to eat with such a one. . . . Is it not those inside the church whom you are to judge?" (1 Cor 5:11–12). In the same letter the Apostle shows himself to be perplexed that no one in the church feels competent to decide a case among brothers who hence proceed to take it to a worldly judge: "When one of you has a grievance against a brother, does he dare go to law before the unrighteous instead of the saints? Do you not know that the saints will judge the world? And if the world is to be judged by you, are you incompetent to try trivial cases?" (1 Cor 6:1–2).

Scripture Interpreted by the Tradition

Are there perhaps two irreconcilable positions on judgment in the New Testament? Before denying that Scripture is divinely inspired and thus necessarily free from flagrant contradictions, we may do well to consider how these passages of Sacred Scripture have been read in the Sacred Tradition. There may well be plausible ways of interpreting them as consistent which may help us to understand better what is meant by judgment. Thus, St. John Chrysostom interprets the Matthean formula as an injunction "not to assail with pride, but to correct with tenderness,"[2] reminding us that Christ taught Peter that if his brother sinned against him, he should go and tell him his fault (see Matt 18:15). For Chrysostom, a stricter reading would be incompatible with the nature of the authority that Christ has given to Peter and the apostles: "How gave He them the keys also? Since if they are not to judge, they will be without authority in any matter, and in vain have they received the power to bind and to loose."[3]

"Judge not, that you be not judged" (Matt 7:1). For St. Augustine this command signifies that "in the case of those actions respecting which it is doubtful with what intention they are done, we are to put the better construction on them."[4] This is particularly the case with actions that are in themselves indifferent and thus admit of being done with either good or bad purpose, so that here it would indeed be "rash to judge, especially for the purpose of condemning."[5] However, he also points out that there are actions "which manifestly cannot be done with a good intention; such as debaucheries, or blasphemies . . . and all such things," in which case, Augustine is convinced that "we are permitted to judge."[6]

St. Thomas Aquinas's exposition on judgment is particularly noteworthy. In the context of interpreting verse 1 of chapter 2 of Paul's Letter to the Romans, "Therefore you have no excuse, O man, whoever you are, when you judge another," the Angelic Doctor also discusses Matthew 7:1: "Judge not, that you be not judged." He points out that "this does not mean that every judgment is a cause of condemnation,"[7] distinguishing three kinds of judgment: one that is just, one that is unjust, and one that is rash. While he takes for granted that the reader understands what is meant by a just or unjust judgment, he deems it useful to dedicate a few paragraphs on

2. Chrysostom, *Homilies on Matthew*, XXIII, 2.

3. Ibid., XXIII, 1.

4. Augustine, *Our Lord's Sermon on the Mount*, II, 18, 59.

5. Ibid., II, 18, 60.

6. Ibid., II, 18, 59.

7. Aquinas, *Commentary on the Letter of Paul to the Romans*, Chapter 2, Lesson 1, 174.

the one that is rash. For St. Thomas a judgment is rash on two occasions, namely "when a person passes judgment on a matter committed to him without due knowledge of the truth," or "when a person presumes to judge about hidden matters, of which God alone has the power to judge."[8] Thus, in order to avoid a rash judgment, one must investigate a matter well, making sure to have a sufficient basis in sure knowledge. And some matters of judgment are indeed by their very nature precluded from human reach, inasmuch as they require knowledge that is exclusive to God, such as that about "the thoughts of the heart" and "the contingent future."[9] We simply do not know what went on in the heart of those who acted, nor do we know what will become of them in the future; if they are righteous now, they may still fall; if they are living sinfully now, they may still convert. In his *Commentary on St. Matthew's Gospel*, St. Thomas explains further: While God "has entrusted us with judging externals . . . he has reserved internals to himself. . . . For no one ought to judge that another is an evil man, for doubts must be interpreted in the more favorable light."[10]

We may note that it is this distinction between the external and the internal that allows St. John Paul II to emphasize that "the judgment of one's state of grace obviously belongs only to the person involved, since it is a question of examining one's conscience."[11] Here, in conscience, each person stands or falls before God, who is his or her ultimate master and judge (see Rom 14:4). Yet there are also matters that pertain to externals, which is why the Polish pope continues: "However, in cases of outward conduct which is seriously, clearly and steadfastly contrary to the moral norm, the Church, in her pastoral concern for the good order of the community and out of respect for the sacrament, cannot fail to feel directly involved,"[12] and hence to pass a judgment, not on the person's heart but on the person's outward conduct, which may be such as to bar him or her from the Eucharistic table.

Thus far we have learned from the Scriptures as interpreted by the Tradition that God alone judges the human heart whereas believers, and especially competent authority, can and at times must judge external behavior. If they judge others in a proper manner, they will do so because it is the loving thing to do, for "whoever brings back a sinner from the error of his way will

---

8. Ibid., Chapter 2, Lesson 1, 175.

9. Ibid.

10. Aquinas, *Commentary on St. Matthew's Gospel*, Chapter 7, Lesson 1.

11. John Paul II, *Ecclesia de Eucharistia*, no. 37.

12. Ibid.

save his soul from death and will cover a multitude of sins" (Jas 5:20). Yet a further question arises, namely that of the state of the one who admonishes. Here, it is interesting to note that for St. Augustine, the possibility of "judging" fellow believers, that is, of pointing out their sin to them and calling them to conversion, does not depend on the righteousness of the one who is giving the exhortation. In other words, for the Doctor of Grace, even a sinner can rightly and without hypocrisy call another sinner to conversion, namely by inviting him or her to join in the common effort of conversion:

> When necessity shall compel us to find fault with or rebuke any one, we may reflect first whether the fault is such as we have never had, or one from which we have now become free; and if we have never had it, let us reflect that we are men, and might have had it; but if we have had it, and are now free from it, let the common infirmity touch the memory, that not hatred but pity may go before that fault-finding or administering of rebuke. . . . If, however, on reflection, we find ourselves involved in the same fault as he is whom we were preparing to censure, let us not censure nor rebuke; but yet let us mourn deeply over the case, and let us invite him not to obey us, but to join us in a common effort.[13]

St. Thomas puts it this way: if someone is "secretly guilty of the same sin, he does not sin by judging another about the same sin, especially when he does so with humility and with an effort to rise again."[14] Hence, judging, as understood by the church, does not mean to say that one is better than the one whom one judges. It is not a matter of proudly exalting oneself by abasing another, but an attempt to help someone to come back on his or her feet, with "fear and trembling" (see Phil 2:12) and in awareness of one's own need for conversion inasmuch as one is also, always an individual believer, even if perhaps one holds a particular office that requires one to speak in the name of the church as such.

The Challenge of "Weak Thought"

A Univocal Metaphysics

Apart from the objection that the New Testament forbids judgment, which—*pace* Schüssler-Fiorenza—we have shown not to be the case, there

---

13. Augustine, *Our Lord's Sermon on the Mount*, II, 19, 64.

14. Aquinas, *Commentary on the Letter of Saint Paul to the Romans*, Chapter 2, Lesson 1, 177.

is a still more fundamental, philosophical challenge. It is the challenge of so-called "weak thought" that, if admitted, would make any judging impossible, whether it be about internal or external matters. The expression "weak thought" was introduced into the public debate in large degree by the Italian philosopher Gianni Vattimo, and is perhaps more common in Romanic countries than in Anglo-Saxon or German-speaking ones. Nonetheless, it refers to a major challenge for philosophical and theological debate in all Western countries alike. "Weak thought" declares metaphysics obsolete and ultimately denies that human beings have any access to truth. It advocates an incomplete thinking and accuses all those who claim the ability to make reference to God, nature, or reason of being idolaters who have turned God into a being they comprehend. Alternatively, the charge is that of bigotry: those who speak of God and truth and right set themselves up as the voice of reason, while simply masking their own pretenses to which they try to add weight by referring to a higher authority. In the following, we will present the hypothesis that "weak" or "incomplete" thought has its roots in late Scholasticism and ultimately derives from what Brad Gregory aptly calls a "univocal metaphysics."[15]

The issue of weak thought is about whether metaphysics, as a science that reflects about God and being, about substances and natures, is possible or not. Whether or not we think metaphysics as possible will ultimately hinge around the question, sometimes asked in jest: "What do you mean by 'is'?" What does it mean for anything to be and in particular, what does it mean for God to *be*? In his synthesis of Christian thought up to his day, St. Thomas Aquinas proposed an analogical metaphysics that permitted him to affirm that God *is*, but that for him to *be* does not mean the same as it means for us. As Gregory sums it up, "according to Aquinas, God in metaphysical terms was, incomprehensible, *esse*—not a being but the sheer act of to-be, in which all creatures participated insofar as they existed and through which all creation was mysteriously sustained."[16] God is not to be found among the things of this world, he is not an object, not even the highest and most perfect being (*ens*) in the world. God is immanent and at the same time completely transcendent. His mode of being is so different from ours that we cannot grasp it with the concepts of our mind. As Augustine famously says, "If thou hast been able to comprehend it, thou

---

15. See Gregory, *The Unintended Reformation*.
16. Ibid., 38.

hast comprehended something else instead of God."[17] And yet, given that being is not a genus, for St. Thomas it can be predicated analogically even of God, without thereby making him a "thing" within creation, without thereby reducing him to our concepts, turning God into an idol made by our own hands, or at least by our own thought.

With the spreading of William of Ockham's nominalism, by the sixteenth century the thought of an analogical metaphysics was increasingly abandoned. Gregory puts it this way: "In Occamist nominalism . . . insofar as God existed, 'God' had to denote some *thing*, some discrete, real entity, an *ens*."[18] This view had a great historical success, so that "at the outset of the sixteenth century, the dominant scholastic view of God was not *esse* but *ens*—not the incomprehensible act of to-be, but a highest being among other beings."[19] The reasons for this loss do not necessarily have to be sought in any inherent weakness of this idea, unless, perhaps we want to call a certain conceptual complexity a weakness. An external contingent reason was that the Reformers tended to have a preference for nominalism as undermining the authority of the Roman Church, while at the same time possessing an outspoken dislike of analogy as something that they perceived to be strengthening the Catholic case. Thus, a couple of hundred years later, but always speaking from the heart of the Protestant tradition, Karl Barth claimed that the analogy of being was the invention of the Antichrist and the main reason that kept him from becoming a Catholic.[20]

By the beginning of modernity, metaphysics had become univocal, even among many Catholic thinkers. On a univocal metaphysics, saying that God *is*, turns him into the highest being of all the beings in this world, a being that can be grasped by the human mind and thus has lost its transcendence. Such a God is of course highly improbable, which is why Dietrich Bonhoeffer insists that "there is no God who 'is there.'"[21] In the same vein, Gianni Vattimo expresses his hesitancy about attributing existence to God: "What does it mean to say that God exists? Where? Here, or in heaven, or hiding under the table, or only in church?"[22] Along the same

17. Augustine, *Sermons on Selected Lessons of the New Testament*, Sermon 2, 16.

18. Gregory, *Unintended Reformation*, 38 (original emphasis).

19. Ibid.

20. Barth, *Church Dogmatics*, I/1, xiii: "I regard the *analogia entis* as the invention of Antichrist, and I believe that because of it it is impossible ever to become a Catholic."

21. Bonhoeffer, *Act and Being*, 115, as cited in Vattimo and Girard, *Christianity, Truth and Weakening Faith*, 115.

22. Vattimo and Girard, *Christianity, Truth and Weakening Faith*, 54–55.

lines, even a thinker who is Catholic like Jean-Luc Marion prefers to speak of a "God without being."[23]

A univocal metaphysics will not only make it difficult for us to say that God "is" without turning him into an idol, it will also have important repercussions on the notion of truth. For St. Thomas, "true expresses the correspondence of being to the knowing power. . . . This agreement is called 'the conformity of thing and intellect.' In this conformity is fulfilled the formal constituent of the true, and this is what the true adds to being, namely, the conformity or equation of thing and intellect."[24] Truth is the correspondence between the intellect and reality or the being of things. An opinion is true if it corresponds to the way things are; it is false if it does not correspond to reality. The question that remains open is of course: Which way are things? The things judge the human intellect, but how are they? Who judges the criteria that judge the human mind? This is where the transcendent God comes into play. Even in the case of the divine intellect, truth is a relationship between intellect and things. Only, now it is not the divine intellect that is judged by things, but rather things are judged by God's intellect: "Natural things from which our intellect gets its scientific knowledge measure our intellect. Yet these things are themselves measured by the divine intellect, in which are all created things—just as all works of art find their origin in the intellect of an artist."[25] It is God's knowledge that makes all things, and things are "true" or "false" to the extent they correspond to the idea, to the plan that he has for them: "A natural thing . . . is said to be true with respect to the conformity with the divine intellect in so far as it fulfills the end to which it was ordained by the divine intellect."[26] The way things are, which is the criterion that judges the human intellect, is judged by the divine intellect. The truth of things lies in the way God knows them. Inasmuch as God is transcendent and inasmuch as his knowledge is creative, his judgment of things is not conditioned by any particular perspective, whereas ours necessarily is. He alone knows things the way they really are, since he made them and since he transcends them. Without God's intellect judging things by knowing them, there would be no truth of things; there would be no ultimate criterion for "the way things are" and hence neither could the human intellect be judged by "the way things are."

23. See Marion, *God Without Being*.
24. Aquinas, *Truth*, I, 1.
25. Ibid., I, 2.
26. Ibid.

31

Now on a univocal metaphysics that makes God a being among beings, God's view on things, i.e., his judgment of them, would be as relative and conditioned as any other judgment. A perspective from within this world is always a particular perspective. On account of this perspectivity, God's intellect could no longer judge all things as they are in themselves. According to Robert Spaemann, this intricate relationship between a transcendent God and truth was well seen by Friedrich Nietzsche who wrote in his *The Gay Science:* "It is still a *metaphysical faith* upon which our faith in science rests—that even we knowers of today, we godless anti-metaphysicians, still take *our* fire, too, from the flame lit by the thousand-year old faith, the Christian faith which was also Plato's faith, that God is truth; that truth is divine."[27] Spaemann comments this passage in the following way: "If there is no God, Nietzsche writes, then there is no such thing as truth. Then there are only subjective perspectives in the world, but there is no such thing as a true world beyond these perspectives. Only when there is the universal glance of God, God's universal perspective, from which the world derived, then there is such a thing as an absolute, unchangeable truth. If there is *no* truth in this sense, then there is no Enlightenment, and then the Enlightenment, by abolishing God, destroys itself. This was precisely Nietzsche's conviction."[28] This, as Spaemann points out, is also Richard Rorty's position, whom he cites on a different occasion. Rorty says, "There would only be a 'higher' aim of inquiry called 'truth' if there were such a thing as ultimate justification—justification before God, or before the tribunal of reason, as opposed to any merely finite human audience."[29]

If there is no God that transcends any partial perspective and whose intellect contains and judges all things, then any human claim to truth would have to be arrogant. As Vattimo says, "It's absolute certainties that have got us where we are now, speaking of tragedies. So let's get rid of them altogether, these truths!"[30] Indeed, some pages down Vattimo goes on exclaiming, "Jesus Christ has set me free from belief in idols, in divinities, in natural laws, and so on, and so in this sense I define myself as an atheist. But an atheist only with respect to the God of philosophers, obviously, meaning

27. Nietzsche, *Gay Science*, 201 (original emphases).

28. Spaemann, "Wahrheit und Freiheit," 329 (my own translation, original emphasis).

29. Rorty, *Philosophy and Social Hope*, 38. See Spaemann, "Gottesbeweise nach Nietzsche," 45.

30. Vattimo and Girard, *Christianity, Truth and Weakening Faith*, 42.

God as 'pure act,' 'omniscience,' and so on."[31] If we are convinced that there is no transcendent judge of truth and falsity, whether we are atheists of the strict observance or whether we thank God for our being atheists,[32] it will necessarily seem to us that any human being who affirms, "this is *true*," intending to refer to something objective, would set him- or herself up as the ultimate arbiter of all reality. We should want to recommend some more humility, as does Paolo Flores d'Arcais in one of his highly polemical writings: "We have already encountered in passing the clerical cunning with which one passes for 'natural law' one's own morality and one's own debatable life style, which one intends to turn into law, depriving others of liberty."[33] A reference to the truth of things would add nothing to an expression of personal preference or desire except a claim to the absolutization of this preference or desire. It would mean to put an exclamation mark behind the "I want!" and tyrannically seek to exclude all other opinions or preferences. Questions of "truth" and "falsity" would thus have to be negotiated in the same way as questions of likes and dislikes. This is why Richard Rorty can suggest to think of truth in terms of solidarity,[34] while Gianni Vattimo would prefer to speak of truth as charity: "It is still possible to speak of truth, you understand, but only because we have realized *caritas* through agreement. *Caritas* with respect to opinion, with respect to choices about values, will become the truth when it is shared."[35]

The question, then, is when and why we have "killed God," as Nietzsche put it,[36] and with him metaphysics, nature, reason. I would like to suggest that we "killed God" when we introduced a univocal metaphysics. In other words, if there is any "murderer" of God, his name is Ockham

31. Ibid., 53.

32. See ibid.

33. Flores d'Arcais, "*La democrazia*," 108 (original emphases; my own translation).

34. Rorty, "Solidarity or Objectivity?" 169: "Those who wish to ground solidarity in objectivity—call them 'realists'—have to construe truth as correspondence to reality. So they must construct a metaphysics that has room for a special relation between beliefs and objects which will differentiate true from false beliefs. . . . By contrast, those who wish to reduce objectivity to solidarity—call them 'pragmatists'—do not require a metaphysics or an epistemology. They view truth as, in William James's phrase, what is good for *us* to believe. . . . From a pragmatist point of view, to say that what is rational for us now to believe may not be *true*, is simply to say that somebody may come up with a better idea" (original emphases).

35. Vattimo and Girard, *Christianity, Truth and Weakening Faith*, 51.

36. See Nietzsche, *Gay Science*, 120: "God is dead! God remains dead! And we have killed him! How can we console ourselves, the murderers of all murderers!"

rather than Nietzsche. It was this God of the univocal metaphysics of late scholasticism and modernity whose death Nietzsche announced, but he was not really murdered but died of weakness and old age. The force of Martin Heidegger's charge against all metaphysics since Socrates as onto-theology and as being forgetful of being rests on a univocal metaphysics that indeed thinks of being-as-such (*esse*) as a being (*ente*) among beings and calls this being "God," who undeniably would be a God before whom "man can neither fall to his knees in awe nor . . . play music and dance."[37] Gregory formulates it this way: "Heidegger sensed but seems not to have seen that the 'forgetfulness of being' (*Seinsvergessenheit*) pertained not so much to a Christian understanding of God but only to a univocal metaphysics, which, especially since the advent of medieval nominalism, has indeed tended toward a recurrence of the ancient pagan conception of god(s) as the highest being(s) *within* the universe."[38] Afraid of turning being-as-such (*esse*) into a particular being (*ens*), the only solution Heidegger saw was to *turn being into becoming* and ultimately in a paradoxically productive "Nothing," resulting in an *idea of truth as "needless" freedom*. This, at least, is the interpretation that in his monumental work on the analogy of being Erik Przywara proposes of Heidegger's thought:

> In Heidegger's existential phenomenology . . . both the absolute of being and the absolute of truth give way to the pure becoming of a creature incurvated upon itself (as shaped by "care" "in the world"). Just as being comes to mean becoming, truth comes to mean a "needless [*notgewendet*] freedom." . . . The Hegelian "contradiction" has been radicalized in the Heideggerian "Nothing." But this Nothing, as Nothing, is the fundamental principle determining and producing all things.[39]

Our present proposal is this one: could it be that we have not killed, but merely forgotten the true God? Could it be that while, granting to Heidegger that this God would certainly not be a being among beings, there could still be a meaningful, namely analogical, way of speaking about him, which would allow us to ascribe existence to him without turning him into an idol? Could this God not be the condition for the possibility of there being a truth that no human being can possess or grasp completely, but that is nonetheless objective, having as its standard the absolute intellect

---

37. Heidegger, "Onto-theo-logical Constitution of Metaphysics," 72.

38. Gregory, *Unintended Reformation*, 65 (original emphasis).

39. Przywara, *Analogia Entis: Metaphysics*, 202.

of God, and that humans can approach and share in—as "in a mirror dimly" (see 1 Cor 13:12), and yet truly? Could it not be that this God has indeed a plan for his creatures, the first indications of which he has written in their nature? And is this idea that beings have natures really all that implausible? Even the most convinced nominalists tend to speak of human beings, dogs, bears and lions, all of which are universal terms the meaningfulness of which is denied by nominalism. And even if the nominalist were to reply that these terms are just conventional, based on family-resemblance, he or she would still tend to deal with a full-grown tiger differently than with a cat, any family resemblance notwithstanding, practically admitting that there is something in a tiger's and a cat's very being (i.e., their "nature") that warrants such a differentiated treatment. Thus, in brief, a first response to "weak thought" is this: One may grant that the problem to which "weak thought" tries to respond is a real one. A univocal metaphysics turns God into an idol, whereupon claims to objective truth may easily become little-veiled affirmations of one's own will. Its solution, the abolition of *any* metaphysics may just be too high a price to pay, given that one could look for an alternative, ultimately more plausible solution in a quest to rediscover an analogical metaphysics.

The Medical Analogy

A second, somewhat less complex, observation about "weak thought" and judgment may well be in order. Even proponents of weak thought, one may suppose, would go to the medical doctor when they feel physically unwell. Even Paolo Flores d'Arcais, who claims that "natures" are cunningly devised by clerics to impose their will on the faithful,[40] would presumably have the sense that going several days in a row at a body-temperature of 102°F is an indication of a physical problem, even though theoretically he would have no grounds for doing so. Notice how the affirmation "Healthy human beings have a body temperature of about 98.6°F" implies a presupposition about human nature (a universal) and a judgment about a truth with respect to that nature. If there is no human nature, what will keep me from assuming that perhaps my own best body temperature lies at 95°F or at 101°F? Of course, when I'm at 102°F, I may feel pretty bad, but what would it even mean to feel "bad" without any standard of feeling "good"? And would not a medical doctor assessing my temperature at 104°F immediately

40. See again: Flores d'Arcais, "*La democrazia,*" 108.

take measures to lower it, even if I did not complain that I felt weak or uncomfortable? The medical science can work only if it presupposes a human nature that implies certain standards of proper or improper functioning of the organism. In trying to help sick persons, doctors judge them in many ways, and no one blames them for trying to exalt themselves and their own health by debasing others, nor for claiming to find the ultimate standard for right or wrong in their own arbitrary will.

Doctors first judge that there is indeed something wrong with a patient. Then they proceed to make a diagnosis. When they tell the patient: "You have diabetes," this judgment neither serves to exalt the doctors nor to debase the patient. It is a judgment that is meant to heal. Indeed, medical science is highly advanced; yet it can only heal if the proper diagnosis is made preferably at the opportune time. Is the diagnostic judgment always right? No, a doctor may get it wrong. But from the mere fact that at times a judgment is wrong, no one would come to the conclusion that in matters of physical health, the question of truth or falsity is not applicable, that there *is* no right or wrong. It is precisely the fact that a judgment may be wrong which indicates that truth and falsity apply to it. Wrong things can be said about an issue only if true things, too, can be said.

We must also consider that medical doctors do not only judge about possible illnesses, but also about actual lifestyles. They will say, "Drinking a bottle of whiskey a day is not good for you," or "Physical exercise will benefit your health." But who are they to judge? Well, they have studied the human organism; they believe that, at least in terms of organic life, there is such a thing as human nature; they believe that in their organism human beings are more or less wired the same way, which justifies them in pronouncing such general judgments. Doctors will of course keep in mind a person's sex, age, and general constitution, but this would not keep them from affirming that too much alcohol or smoking are bad and that exercise is good for health. Also this could be quite independent from their own personal conduct. They may be drinking quite a bit and still be saying the same things, because they believe that the truth of these affirmations does not depend on them.

Now if we are inclined to believe that there exists something like truth or falsity in our bodies, that is, in the physical aspect of our nature, why would it be implausible to look for truth and falsity also in the spiritual aspect of our nature, i.e., in our relationships? Can a relationship between a human being and God, between a husband and his wife, between a mother and her children, not be in a healthy or unhealthy state? Can we not speak of acts that always and everywhere hurt a relationship just as smoking always hurts the organism?

Vattimo advocates charity as the overall rule and on top of this proposes what he calls "traffic rules" to prevent hurting others: "Ever fewer idols, ever more 'atheism.' No natural proofs of God, only charity and, of course, ethics. I always say that ethics is merely charity plus the traffic regulations. I respect the rules of the road because I don't want to cause the death of my neighbor and because I ought to love him. But to suppose that there is something about running a red light that goes against nature is ridiculous."[41] One may grant that traffic regulations are somewhat conventional and are useful to the extent that they indeed help us to keep safe on the road. But no one who advocates natural law would claim that running a light goes against nature. Natural law is much more fundamental,[42] so fundamental that even Vattimo presupposes it without noticing. In what he says, he presupposes that risking the death of my neighbor is opposed to charity. What permits him to do so? Here, natural law comes in as something that I do not need to learn but originally find in me. I originally know that life is good, and that if I want to love people—if I want their good—then I need to respect their lives, for instance. If really everything were as relative as Vattimo claims in other places, if really "God can only be a relativist,"[43] then we could not even say as much, namely that to love someone implies to respect his or her life. Just as our organism wants to keep our body temperature at around 98.6°F, the spiritual or rational part of us originally wants to respect the life of others, only that this latter aim is entrusted to our freedom in a way that the former is not: it is not only a fact but also a task. Respect for other people's lives belongs to the "health" of our relationships. In any case, this respect, too, is a "law" of our nature and cannot be reduced to a merely conventional "traffic rule."

Common Sense: The Basis of Judgment

Common Sense and Judgment in Kant and Arendt

Having dealt with the possible scriptural and philosophical objections against the possibility of judgment and the belief that judging is both

41. Vattimo and Girard, *Christianity, Truth and Weakening Faith*, 35.

42. See the ample interdisciplinary study on the topic of natural law found in Berkman and Mattison, eds., *Searching for a Universal Ethic*.

43. Vattimo and Girard, *Christianity, Truth and Weakening Faith*, 48.

permitted and possible, we now have to consider a third question that is by no means trivial, namely the question of how to judge well. We have argued that judgment is not an act of the will (in which case it would be indifferent to truth or falsity), but that it is an act of the intellect whereby the intellect conforms to reality, though not infallibly so. To see how one can reduce the real possibility of error in judging, we will turn to Hannah Arendt's discussion of common sense, which is inspired by Immanuel Kant.

We have all been wrong before, giving a wrong judgment, a wrong "diagnosis" about what we thought to be the case, about another person or about ourselves. Sometimes we overhear just fragments of a conversation, our mind supplying the rest based on our prior expectations. How much did we really hear, and how much did we simply think we heard? Indeed at times we do well to question our judgment. And yet we must ask on which basis. Isn't any questioning of our judgment just another judgment? Here, for Hannah Arendt, common sense in its Kantian meaning comes in. We read in Kant's *Critique of Judgement*:

> By the name *sensus communis* is to be understood the idea of a public sense, i.e., a critical faculty which in its reflective act takes account (a priori) of the mode of representation of everyone else, in order, as it were, to weigh its judgement with the collective reason of mankind, and thereby avoid the illusion arising from subjective and personal conditions which could readily be taken for objective, an illusion that would exert a prejudicial influence upon its judgement. This is accomplished by weighing the judgement, not so much with actual, as rather with the merely possible, judgements of others, and by putting ourselves in the position of everyone else.[44]

For Kant, when common sense expresses judgments on a matter, it takes into account the way others think about the issue, in some way reaching up to "the collective reason of mankind."

Kant, to be sure, was not known for his field research. For him, one can take others into account by considering their potential and not necessarily their actual judgments. It is enough to place myself in the position of others, thinking "from the standpoint of everyone else." I do not "count noses" as Arendt puts it, who is indeed able to find a convincing example that shows that Kant's "enlarged mentality"[45] does not always need to be the result of a survey of people's opinions:

44. Kant, *Critique of Judgement*, 123 (§ 40).

45. See Kant, *Critique of Judgement*, 124 (§ 40). The "enlarged mentality," as Arendt

> Suppose I look at a specific slum dwelling and I perceive in this particular building the general notion which it does not exhibit directly, the notion of poverty and misery. I arrive at this notion by representing to myself how I would feel if I had to live there, that is, I try to think in the place of the slum-dweller. The judgment I shall come up with will by no means necessarily be the same as that of the inhabitants whom time and hopelessness may have dulled to the outrage of their condition, but it will become an outstanding example for my further judging of these matters. Furthermore, while I take into account others when judging, this does not mean that I conform in my judgment to theirs.[46]

People living in misery may indeed be "dulled to the outrage of their condition." If I were to ask them how they are doing, they might just say that all was fine. For me to think in their place means to think how "I would feel if I had to live there"—it is not necessary to take opinion polls in this case.

Nonetheless, in his discussion of common sense, Kant does seem to imply that for him the privileged access to the world is his own mind. Arendt, in contrast, is more concrete and practical, even though in her own view she is simply interpreting Kant. She insists that the reason why common sense is called "common" is not based on the fact that it simply happens to be common to all of us. Rather, it is common inasmuch as it "fits us into a community with others, makes us members of it and enables us to communicate things given by our five private senses."[47] Given the capacity of the imagination, common sense can indeed "have present in itself all those who actually are absent."[48] But for Arendt, in contrast to Kant, those "who actually are absent" are indeed real people, whose judgments on similar occasions I am familiar with, whom I know and with whom in some ways I share my life. Thus, "when somebody makes the judgment, this is beautiful, he does not mean merely to say this pleases me . . . but he claims assent from others because in judging he has already taken them into account and hence hopes that his judgments will carry a certain general, though perhaps not universal, validity."[49] Common sense makes sure

---

usually renders Kant's "*erweiterte Denkungsart*," or the "broadened mind," as it is translated in the present English edition, is the result of putting ourselves in the position of others.

46. Arendt, "Some Questions of Moral Philosophy," 140–41.

47. Ibid., 139.

48. Ibid., 140.

49. Ibid.

our judgments are not based on our individual whims. If I judge a particular painting or piece of music as beautiful, my judgment is confirmed by my friends who likewise find it beautiful. And even if one day I walk alone through a museum, my friends will in some way be present through my imagination. I know their taste and I can imagine their judgment and will take their judgment into account. The common sense of the community of which we are a part greatly influences our judgment, in all aspects of our lives, whether in politics, science, aesthetics or morals.

There are moments, even in making judgments about ourselves, when it is reasonable to trust the judgment of others more than our own, especially if they know us well or possess an expert knowledge on particular issues. This is why Alasdair MacIntyre writes, "What is or would be good or best for me is something on which, apart from the fact that generally and characteristically I know more about myself than others do, I may in many and crucial respects be no more of an authority than some others and in some respects a good deal less of an authority than some others. My physician, or my trainer, if I am an athlete, or my teacher, if I am a student, may well be better placed to make judgments about my good than I am."[50] My judgment is always influenced by the community of which I am a part, and it is also very reasonable that it be so. In order to grow up and come of age, what we need to do is not to isolate ourselves and ward ourselves off from any influence of others. This is neither realistically possible nor practically helpful. What we can and should do is to discriminate in choosing the people who influence us. Here, Arendt puts great emphasis on the examples and role models that guide our lives,[51] while Livio Melina insists that "the first and fundamental moral choice is the choice of our friends."[52] According to Arendt, the validity of judgment "will reach as far as the community of which common sense makes me a member."[53] Kant, no doubt, was very optimistic about this. Thinking himself a "citizen of the world," he

50. MacIntyre, *Dependent Rational Animals*, 71.

51. See Arendt, "Some Questions of Moral Philosophy," 145: "We judge and tell right from wrong by having present in our mind some incident and some person, absent in time or space, that have become examples. There are many such examples. They can lie far back in the past or they can be among the living. They need not be historically real; as Jefferson once remarked: 'the fictitious murder of Duncan by Macbeth' excites in us 'as great a horror of villainy, as the real one of Henri IV' and a 'lively and lasting sense of filial duty is more effectually impressed on a son or daughter by reading King Lear, than by all the dry volumes of ethics and divinity that ever were written.'"

52. Melina, *Sharing in Christ's Virtues*, 31.

53. Arendt, "Some Questions of Moral Philosophy," 140.

"hoped it would reach to the community of all mankind."[54] But even if this side of heaven there are different communit*ies*, all of which differ in their judgments on certain issues, the fact remains that "the community among men produces a common sense. The validity of common sense grows out of the intercourse with people."[55] For Arendt, this common sense, "is the mother of judgment," so that "not even a painting or a poem, let alone a moral issue, can be judged without invoking and weighing silently the judgment of others just as I refer to the schema of the bridge to recognize other bridges."[56]

To say that common sense, the sense that is produced by the community of which we are a part, is the mother of judgment does not at all mean that judgment is relative or arbitrary. It simply means that we have to choose our community well. This may also be the meaning of Cicero's affirmation that he would much rather "be mistaken with Plato . . . than be in the right with those others,"[57] i.e., with the Pythagoreans. The contradiction with the classical Latin adage "Amicus Plato, sed magis amica veritas—Plato is a friend but truth is a greater friend"[58] may be a seeming one only. Most certainly "reason prescribes that all men should prefer truth to their friends,"[59] and Cicero may not actually intend here to subject truth to friendship,[60] but rather to suggest that we are more likely to arrive at truth if we stay in the company of someone we can trust. We need to judge our judgment. In whose company will our judgment place us? If our judgment on a certain issue implies that Plato, whom we admire, is wrong and that those whose opinions we usually disdain are right, then it may actually be more *reasonable* for us to suspend your judgment, part company with these latter and maintain your loyalty to Plato, whom we know to be reliable.

54. Ibid., 140.

55. Ibid., 141.

56. Ibid., 141–42.

57. Cicero, *Tusculan Disputations*, Book I, Chapter 17, 301–2.

58. This saying is often attributed to Aristotle. It paraphrases Aristotle, *Nicomachean Ethics* I, 6, 1096a15: "Still perhaps it would appear desirable, and indeed it would seem to be obligatory, especially for a philosopher, to sacrifice even one's closest personal ties in defence of the truth."

59. Aquinas, *Commentary on Aristotle's Nicomachean Ethics*, I, Lecture 6, 76.

60. This is actually Hannah Arendt's reading of Cicero's statement: "It is matter of taste to prefer Plato's company and the company of his thoughts even if this should lead us astray from truth" ("Crisis of Culture," 221). While it is possible to understand it this way, we suggest that a different interpretation is thinkable, too.

Our best bet at getting at the truth may at times be to stay with Plato and to avoid the company of others.

The *Sensus Fidelium* as the Church's Common Sense

Thus for Kant and for Arendt judgment is based on common sense which both constitutes and derives from a given community. Now evidently the church, too, is a community, and she, too, has a common sense that is at the basis of ecclesial judgment. In the last part of this chapter, we would like to suggest that one does not need to look far to find the church's common sense. We would like to propose that this common sense that distinguishes the members of the ecclesial community and permits them to judge well, is found in the idea of the *sensus fidei* or *sensus fidelium* of which the Second Vatican Council speaks, implicitly basing itself on the writings of John Henry Cardinal Newman.[61]

What did the fathers of the Second Vatican Council, or Cardinal Newman for that matter, mean by the *sensus fidei* or the *sensus fidelium*? At times the "sense of the faith" or the "sense of the faithful" is understood to be something that appertains specifically to the laity, that is, to those who are not ordained and who have not taken religious vows. Indeed Cardinal Newman's historical examples in *On Consulting the Faithful in Matters of Doctrine* (the Arian crisis of the fourth century and the definition of the dogma of the Immaculate Conception) do suggest a certain polarity here, at least between the laity and bishops. According to the English Cardinal, during the Arian crisis it was the common believers who upheld the church's faith as proclaimed at the Council of Nicaea, while many of the bishops became unfaithful for political reasons.[62] Before defining the dogma of the Immaculate Conception, Pope Pius IX made it a point to consult the manners ordinary Christians honored the Blessed Virgin.[63] Thus, in the first

61. See John Henry Newman, *On Consulting the Faithful*.

62. See ibid., 75–76: "It is not a little remarkable, that, though, historically speaking, the fourth century is the age of doctors . . . nevertheless in that very day the divine tradition committed to the infallible Church was proclaimed and maintained far more by the faithful than by the Episcopate. . . . In that time of immense confusion the divine dogma of our Lord's divinity was proclaimed, enforced, maintained, and (humanly speaking) preserved, far more by the '*Ecclesia docta*' than by the '*Ecclesia docens*'; that the body of the episcopate was unfaithful to its commission, while the body of the laity was faithful to its baptism."

63. Ibid., 104–5: "In most cases when a definition is contemplated, the laity will have

example there is a clear tension between the laity's sense of the faith and the wavering of the bishops. In the second example there is no tension but nonetheless a polarity between the laity and the pope as representative of the Catholic Church's Magisterium.

Vatican II's Dogmatic Constitution on the Church *Lumen Gentium* clearly bases itself on Newman's thought, though it does not cite him and does not actually speak of "*sensus fidelium*—the sense of the faithful" but rather of the "*sensus fidei*—the sense of the faith." It mentions the *sensus fidei* in two places, in its no. 12 and its no. 35. In the latter instance, on a superficial reading, one may get the impression that the *sensus fidei* is something that belongs to the laity in particular. We read: "Christ . . . fulfils this prophetic office not only by the hierarchy . . . but also by the laity. He accordingly both establishes them as witnesses and provides them with the appreciation of the faith (*sensus fidei*) and the grace of the word."[64] Evidently, the mere affirmation that the laity have the appreciation of the faith does not as such mean that this appreciation is something exclusive to them, just as the grace of the word could hardly be restricted to them. Yet, given that the document speaks of *sensus fidei* only in two places and given that in the second case this expression is used in the context of a discussion of the laity, some have concluded that it had to be understood as an attribute peculiar to those of the faithful who are neither ordained nor professed.[65] This would of course be entirely illogical. How could anyone acquire a specific attribute simply by *not* doing something, that is by simply not getting ordained or taking religious vows? It would mean that clerics and religious, at the moment of their ordination or profession,

---

a testimony to give; but if ever there be an instance when they ought to be consulted, it is in the case of doctrines which bear directly upon devotional sentiments. . . . And the Blessed Virgin is preeminently an object of devotion; and therefore it is, I repeat, that though Bishops had already spoken in favour of her absolute sinlessness, the Pope was not content without knowing the feelings of the faithful."

64. Second Vatican Council, *Lumen Gentium*, no. 35.

65. See for instance Osborne, *Permanent Diaconate*, 121, who suggests that theology has commonly understood the *sensus fidelium* as the voice of laypeople: "In theology . . . the phrase *sensus fidelium*—the sense of the faithful—has usually been interpreted as the voice of the laypeople. Although the term *sensus fidelium* has had many differing interpretations, it has consistently been an honored theological principle. It means that the laypeople have a sort of intuitive understanding of God's presence in a given situation." If this were the meaning of *sensus fidelium*, one should much rather speak of *sensus laicorum*.

would *lose* the *sensus fidei* they had before inasmuch as they were laity up to that point but no longer thereafter.

To understand better what Vatican II means by *sensus fidei*, and to give sustenance to our thesis that the *sensus fidei* could be read in terms of the church's Arendtian "common sense," we need to look at *Lumen Gentium* no. 12:

> The whole body of the faithful who have an anointing that comes from the holy one (cf. 1 Jn. 2:20 and 27) cannot err in matters of belief. This characteristic is shown in the supernatural apprecia- tion of the faith (*sensus fidei*) of the whole people, when, "from the bishops to the last of the faithful" they manifest a universal consent in matters of faith and morals. By this appreciation of the faith, aroused and sustained by the Spirit of truth, the People of God, guided by the sacred teaching authority (magisterium), and obeying it, receives not the mere word of men, but truly the word of God (cf. 1 Th. 2:13).[66]

Here the Council clearly speaks of the "whole body of the faithful," of which also bishops, priests, and religious would seem to be a part. To eradicate any doubt about the matter, the passage continues by speaking of the "whole people," explicitly also including bishops. The *sensus fidei* is thus nothing exclusive to the laity, but it is the "appreciation of the faith" that is "aroused and sustained by the Spirit of truth" and that belongs to the whole People of God.

Thus we need to underline that the sense of the faith belongs to the whole church, which includes the laity, but also the bishops, priests, and religious. This supernatural appreciation of the faith belongs to those of the faithful who are indeed faithful, "guided by sacred teaching authority . . . and obeying it." It is not something that could be ascertained by looking at majority opinions proposed by sociological surveys.[67] It is true that Pius IX consulted the sense of the faithful regarding doctrine, namely before defin- ing the dogma of the Immaculate Conception. But, as Newman puts it, the pope consulted the faithful not in the way one consults with one's advisors, but as one consults a watch:

---

66. Second Vatican Council, *Lumen Gentium*, no. 12.

67. See Francis, "Address to Members of the International Theological Commis- sion": "Of course, it is clear that the *sensus fidelium* must not be confused with the socio- logical reality of majority opinion."

Now doubtless, if a divine were expressing himself formally, and in Latin, he would not commonly speak of the laity being "consulted" among the preliminaries of a dogmatic definition, because the technical, or even scientific, meaning of the word "consult" is to "consult *with*," or to "take *counsel*." But the English word "consult" . . . includes the idea of inquiring into a matter of *fact*, as well as asking a judgment. . . . We may consult a watch or a sun-dial about the time of day. A physician consults the pulse of his patient; but not in the same sense in which his patient consults *him*. It is but an index of the state of his health.[68]

Pope Pius IX did not want to establish the majority opinion, nor did he seek the laity's advice. He rather sought to ascertain their practice—according to the old adage *lex orandi, lex credendi*. What do those of the faithful who are faithful believe in regards to something that had not yet been defined as a dogma? How do they pray? Is there a cult of the Immaculate Virgin among the faithful? What was being consulted was not a theological opinion but a pious practice. We see that Pius IX did not hold an opinion poll. He did not indifferently ask all the baptized—faithful or not to their baptismal vows—what they thought about possibly updating a well-established dogma, say, the divinity of Christ, but rather asked those of the faithful who had cultivated a prayer life whether they cherished the veneration of the Immaculata.

Hence we see that it is impossible to get at the sense of the faith by taking polls because these cannot distinguish between those of the faithful who are faithful and those who are unfaithful. A survey could possibly make baptism a criterion, but unfortunately, not all baptized are faithful to their baptismal vows. However, there is still a further reason for why an opinion poll is of little use here. It can only survey the opinions of those who happen to be alive today, while *Lumen Gentium* speaks of the sense of the faith of the "whole body of the faithful" and of the "whole people." Inasmuch as this "body" is an organism that in some ways extends the Incarnation of Christ in time,[69] it consists not only of those who are

68. Newman, *On Consulting the Faithful*, 54 (original emphases).

69. See John Paul II, *Redemptoris Mater*, no. 5: "The reality of the Incarnation finds a sort of extension in the mystery of the Church—the Body of Christ." See also the groundbreaking work by Johann Adam Möhler, first published in 1843: "The ultimate reason of the visibility of the Church is to be found in the *incarnation* of the Divine Word. . . . But since the Word became flesh, it expressed itself in an outward, perceptible, and human manner. . . . And as in the world nothing can attain to greatness but in society; so Christ established a community. . . . And thus a living, well-connected, visible association of

alive now, but also of those who have gone before. The "People of God" includes every baptized from the times of the Apostles until today. Surveys necessarily miss this element of perdurance in time—the diachronic element—of the *sensus fidei*. William Levada, the eventual successor of Joseph Ratzinger as the Head of the Congregation for the Doctrine of the Faith, points to this fact in an article published in the 1980s, but it is still highly relevant today as it acutely exposes the inconsistencies produced by surveys conducted in consecutive years:

> Last summer [1985] *Our Sunday Visitor* carried the results of a Gallup Poll which had posed the question. "Do you think it is wrong for a man and a woman to have sex relations before marriage or not?" Of the Catholics who responded (50 percent described themselves as regular Massgoers), 33 percent said they believe premarital sex to be wrong, while 59 percent saw it as acceptable. ... On the other hand, in 1969, 72 percent of the Catholics who responded to the poll said they thought premarital sex was wrong. Does this poll constitute a *sensus fidelium*? Has the Holy Spirit guided the *sensus fidelium* from 1969 to 1985 into a total reversal of values? Such a notion strikes me as suspect. Rather than accuse the Holy Spirit of lack of fidelity to the Gospel, it seems to me that we should analyze the data as indicating the enormous invasion of secular values.[70]

The *sensus fidelium* is not constituted simply by the majority opinion of those who are now living. It refers to the sense, the "appreciation"—not the opinion—of all those of the faithful who are or were faithful, whether now living or gone before. It is, as Pope Francis says, "a kind of 'spiritual instinct,'" which allows the members of the church "to *sentire cum Ecclesia* and to discern what conforms to the Apostolic faith and to the spirit of the Gospel."[71] This is why in order to get at the sense of the faithful, the common sense of the church, we cannot look exclusively at the present, but must include the past as it is given to us in Sacred Tradition, as one of the

---

the faithful sprang up, whereof it might be said,—there they are, there is his Church, his institution, wherein he continueth to live, his spirit continueth to work, and the word uttered by him eternally resounds. Thus, the visible Church, from the point of view here taken, is the Son of God himself, everlastingly manifesting himself among men in a human form, perpetually renovated, and eternally young—the permanent incarnation of the same, as in Holy Writ, even the faithful, are called 'the body of Christ'" (*Symbolism*, 5–6, original emphasis).

70. Levada, "Dissent and the Catholic Religion Teacher," 150.

71. Francis, "Address to Members of the International Theological Commission."

ways in which the sense of the faith is expressed. G. K. Chesterton defines tradition as "the democracy of the dead." He goes on explaining:

> Tradition refuses to submit to the small and arrogant oligarchy of those who merely happen to be walking about. All democrats object to men being disqualified by the accident of birth; tradition objects to their being disqualified by the accident of death. Democracy tells us not to neglect a good man's opinion, even if he is our groom; tradition asks us not to neglect a good man's opinion, even if he is our father. I, at any rate, cannot separate the two ideas of democracy and tradition; it seems evident to me that they are the same idea.[72]

Hence, to judge well, informed by an ecclesial common sense, we cannot look exclusively at the present. The community of which the ecclesial common sense makes us a member is larger than the church that is now present. It also includes the church of the past, her tradition, since she is one body, an organism that by divine assistance lives from the moment of her institution by Christ all the way to Christ's coming in glory.

In the document on the *sensus fidei*, the International Theological Commission included an overview of the way this notion has been understood from the Patristic period to our own times. In this context it mentions not only the work of John Henry Newman, but also that of Johann Adam Möhler, whose position it summarizes in the following way:

> Johann Adam Möhler sought to portray the Church as a living organism and to grasp the principles that governed the development of doctrine. In his view, it is the Holy Spirit who animates, guides, and unites the faithful as a community in Christ, bringing about in them an ecclesial "consciousness" of the faith (*Gemeingeist* or *Gesamtsinn*). . . . This *sensus fidei*, which is the subjective dimension of Tradition, necessarily includes an objective element, the Church's teaching, for the Christian "sense" of the faithful, which lives in their hearts and is virtually equivalent to Tradition, is never divorced from its content.[73]

72. Chesterton, *Orthodoxy*, 53.

73. International Theological Commission, *Sensus Fidei*, no. 35. It may be worthwhile citing Möhler directly: "The Church is the body of the Lord: it is, in its universality, His visible form—His permanent, ever-renovated humanity—His eternal revelation. He dwells in the community; all His promises, all His gifts are bequeathed to the community—but to no individual, as such, since the time of the apostles. This general sense, this ecclesiastical consciousness is tradition, in the subjective sense of the word" (*Symbolism*, 35).

It may be worth rediscovering Möhler's insights about the *sensus fidei* being the subjective aspect of tradition, and it may not at all be implausible to relate his discourse about the "general sense" of ecclesial consciousness to the idea of "common sense" as discussed above.

We all need to judge all the time, whether this judgment is about choices concerning our own lives or whether it is about decisions that bear on the larger community. In either case, to judge well, we need to base ourselves on common sense. As we have proposed, the common sense of the church is the *sensus fidei*, that is, the appreciation of the faith that is common to all members of the church throughout the ages and that as such includes tradition. Whenever as Christians we need to judge, discern, or decide, we do well to have our minds informed by this common or general sense. Particularly those of the faithful who have authority in the church and need to judge on matters that directly bear on her life as a whole will find it necessary to consult the *sensus fidelium*—"consult," that is, in Newman's sense, as one "consults a watch"—which means taking into account the convictions and practices of the whole body of Christ, including those of its members who have gone before. The *sensus fidei* is not opposed or juxtaposed to the Sacred Tradition but it is one of the ways the Sacred Tradition expresses itself.[74] In judging, for Kant, "we are suitors for agreement from everyone else,"[75] that is, from all those who are part of our community and whose judgment is a measure for our own judgment.

Thus, when making judgments that regard their own lives or the lives of their families or the workings of their parishes, their dioceses, or the church universal, all members of the church, from the pope and bishops "to the last of the faithful" will need to "woo the consent," as Arendt puts it,[76] not only of all the faithful currently alive, but also of those who have gone before. The church's common sense, the *sensus fidei*, is informed by the judgment of all the popes from Peter to Francis, including Gregory the Great no less than Pius IX, John Paul II and Benedict XVI. It includes the judgments of all the fathers, the doctors, and the saints. We are indeed

---

74. See International Theological Commission, *Sensus Fidei*, no. 66: "As the faith of the individual believer participates in the faith of the Church as a believing subject, so the *sensus fidei (fidelis)* of individual believers cannot be separated from the *sensus fidei (fidelium)* or 'sensus Ecclesiae' of the Church herself, endowed and sustained by the Holy Spirit, and the *consensus fidelium* constitutes a sure criterion for recognising a particular teaching or practice as in accord with the apostolic Tradition."

75. Kant, *Critique of Judgement*, 68 (§19).

76. See Arendt, "Crisis in Culture," 219.

surrounded by a great cloud of witnesses (see Heb 12:1), by many friends whose judgments help to make our own judgments ever sharper and more accurate, whether we are part of the church's teaching office—which in its ministry enjoys the charism of truth by a special assistance of the Holy Spirit—or belong to the last of the faithful. Given that this supernatural appreciation of the faith belongs to the whole body, inasmuch as we are members of this body and in union with it, we can indeed say with St. Paul: "The spiritual man judges all things, but is himself to be judged by no one. 'For who has known the mind of the Lord so as to instruct him?' But we have the mind of Christ" (1 Cor 2:15–16).

3

On Why We Act:
The Question of Teleology

Why Do We Act?

The "Classical" View

WHY DO WE ACT? Why do we do the things we do? The classical Aristotelian doctrine of the four causes indicates four different possible ways in which we may respond to the question, "Why?" If we see a man running in Rome Termini train station and ask ourselves, "Why is he running?" our answer may be:

1. because certain neurons are firing in his brain, giving signals to his muscles, which are moving his legs;

2. because he has muscles and legs;

3. because he is a human being, and running is something human beings do;

4. because he wants to catch a train.

Robert Spaemann and Reinhard Löw point out how only the latter kind of response, that is, the indication of a final cause, allows our curiosity to come to rest, resulting in something we may call understanding.[1] Hence, for Aristotle the final cause was the preeminent one.

However, even upon learning that the man in question is running in order to catch a train, we may still ask why he wants to get on board. Having been informed that he got on the train in order to go to Milan, we may still wonder why he should desire to do so. We may then learn that he is going to Milan in order to meet his fiancé. It is important to note that only at this point, the question "Why?" receives a fully satisfactory answer, that is, when the response is no longer in terms of an "in-order-to" but in terms of a "for-the-sake-of."[2] To understand an action, it is not enough simply to know its instrumental use or utility in a seemingly unending chain of means and ends expressed by the phrase "in order to." When we ask, then, why the man wants to spend time with his fiancé, the answer will (hopefully) not begin with "in order to"—as in: "in order to have some fun"—but rather with: "for the sake of," that is, for her sake, because he loves her. The true final cause of the man's running then, is not the train, nor Milan, but rather his fiancé, whom he loves and who endows his activity with meaningfulness.

We should observe that Aristotle did not restrict final causality to conscious action. For him, the activity of all living beings and indeed of the entire cosmos was to be understood in analogy to the man running for the sake of his beloved. Indeed, the Philosopher says that things seek to maintain themselves in being and to reproduce so as to partake, as far as possible, "in the eternal and divine."[3] As the final cause of all things, God, who for Aristotle is himself unmoved, moves all things as the beloved moves the lover.[4] It is still in this general mindset that Dante, some

1. See Spaemann and Löw, *Natürliche Ziele*, 60: "The final cause holds the primacy in the Aristotelian doctrine of causes. It alone can respond to the question 'why' in the satisfactory sense of leading to understanding" (my own translation).

2. See Arendt, *Human Condition*, 154, for whom the distinction between "in order to" and "for the sake of" corresponds to the distinction between utility and meaningfulness.

3. See Aristotle, *On the Soul*, II, 4, 415a25: "The acts in which it [the nutritive soul] manifests itself are reproduction and the use of food—reproduction, I say, because for any living thing that has reached its normal development and which is unmutilated, and whose mode of generation is not spontaneous, the most natural act is the production of another like itself, an animal producing an animal, a plant a plant, in order that, as far as its nature allows, it may partake in the eternal and divine. That is the goal towards which all things strive, that for the sake of which they do whatsoever their nature renders possible."

4. See Aristotle, *Metaphysics*, XII, 7, 1072b1-5: "The final cause, then, produces motion as being loved."

thousand and six hundred years later, was able to speak of God as that love "which moves the sun and all the other stars."[5] St. Thomas, too, speaks of love as the ultimate for-the-sake-of of any motion in the universe when he says, "every agent, whatever it be, does every action from love of some kind."[6] The word "agent" here is still a very general term, referring to anything that is active, which ultimately means anything that exists, since activity necessarily follows from existence.[7] Thus the Angelic Doctor speaks of a natural love with which a stone is attracted by the center of gravity.[8] The notion of love as something that attracts, i.e., as a kind of gravity, is found also in Augustine who writes, "My love is my weight! I am borne about by it, wheresoever I am borne."[9]

To the classical mind, then, there exists a weight that makes the whole world turn, but not in terms of a material cause but in the sense of a final cause, a love that gives meaning to all existence. The ultimate for-the-sake-of is God, who however allows for the existence of intermediary final causes. The heavens indeed tell the glory of God inasmuch as by their very motion they express their natural "desire" to share in the divine. Why do we and, in fact, all things, act? We act because we love.

An "Inverted Teleology"

How strange all this must sound to the modern and post-modern ear: while what we may choose to call the "classical" position asserts that things strive to maintain themselves in being so they can act for the sake of some love, evolutionism,[10] which applies a systems theory approach to living beings, has long since attempted to convince us that the converse is true. Everything any being does is in function of its self-preservation, which becomes the

---

5. Dante, *Divine Comedy III, Paradiso*, XXXIII, 145. See the very enlightening article by Granados, "Love and the Organism," that begins precisely with this citation.

6. Aquinas, *Summa Theologica*, I-II, 28, 6.

7. See Aquinas, *Summa Contra Gentiles*, I, 43, 2: "From the fact that something is in act it is active." See also Clarke, "Person, Being, and St. Thomas," 603.

8. See Aquinas, *Summa Theologica*, I-II, 26, 1: "The connaturalness of a heavy body for the centre, is by reason of its weight and may be called 'natural love.'"

9. Augustine, *Confessions*, XIII, 9, 10.

10. We should like to distinguish between evolutionism and the theory of evolution. The latter is a distinct scientific paradigm, the former a comprehensive worldview. See Spaemann, "Being and Coming to Be," 166.

ultimate explanatory principle of all motion.[11] Hence, things act and love in order to preserve themselves in being. Here Robert Spaemann speaks of "the inversion of teleology."[12] Things do not act and exist for the sake of some love that transcends them: rather, all they do is geared toward their own preservation in being, which implies expelling all meaningfulness out of existence. Thus, speaking from within this general mindset and arguing "that the fundamental unit of selection, and therefore of self-interest, is not the species, nor the group, nor even, strictly, the individual," but rather "the gene, the unit of heredity,"[13] Richard Dawkins goes on in all earnest to refer to "a mother as a machine programmed to do everything in its power to propagate copies of the genes which ride inside it."[14]

However, some kind of "desire" is still implicitly attributed here to the genes. In conformity with the mechanistic worldview in which it was developed, evolutionism cannot consistently call the self-preservation of the individual, of the species or even of the genes a *goal* of their existence. Rather, on this account it is simply a brute, neutral fact that things that happen to have certain characteristics and act in certain ways have a survival advantage over others. By their own survival, then, they are reinforcing those traits that promoted their survival. But if this view were true, how would one explain the gratuitous beauty to be found in plants and animals, such as the eye-like patterns located on the feathers of the Great Argus, which, according to the biologist Adolf Portmann, have no impact on natural selection?[15] Besides, the rise of human intelligence itself would have to be understood as a simple function of self-preservation, so that reason, as a mere instrument for survival, is seen as the product of "chance and necessity"[16] and thus reduced to the irrational.[17] Inasmuch as on evolutionism's own terms

11. See Spaemann, *Happiness and Benevolence*, 40–50.

12. See ibid., 44: "Modern philosophy begins with what I have . . . called 'the inversion of teleology.' The distinction between living and living well gets flattened out. The content of the well-lived life becomes nothing other than the function of self-preservation."

13. Dawkins, *Selfish Gene*, 11.

14. Ibid., 123.

15. See Portmann, *Aufbruch der Lebensforschung*, 170–87. Also see Portmann's comments on marine snails that express themselves "in a host of splendid forms and colors—each according to its kind. Their appearance speaks a language of which we suspect we can grasp a few words, and gives evidence of a hidden power of life that goes far beyond the needs of mere self-preservation" (*New Paths in Biology*, 159). For a more extensive discussion of Portmann's theses see Kass, "Looking Good," 318–45.

16. See Monod, *Chance and Necessity*.

17. See Pope Benedict XVI's concern that unless we admit that the world, and with

reason's correspondence to reality is accidental, evolutionists cannot claim the truth of their theory. Their theory in fact denies the very possibility of such claims. Evolutionism could give a consistent account of itself only in terms of a theory that is conducive to human survival, but then, of course, nothing is said about its correspondence to reality. To say it in more general terms with Robert Spaemann: "If it were true that acting on conviction was merely a necessary consequence of processes in which the condition of the agent was the chief factor determining the conviction, the account itself could make no claim to be true. . . . A truth-claim could not be taken to mean what it said, but merely noted as a datum of information about the person who made it."[18]

Creators of Value

Why do we act? Classical theory sees an *analogy* between human action and the motion of all things. All things act because they love, even though, of course, what it means for a stone to love is radically different from what it means for a human being to love. Reductionist theories such as evolutionism seek to explain human action and the motion of all things *univocally*. All things ultimately act to keep themselves or their species in being. Human action and the acts of other things are understood exactly in the same way. A man who is running to the train and a stone that is falling down the hill are not doing anything essentially different. However, there is yet a third way of responding to the question of why we act. This response sees a radical *equivocation* between the activity of human beings and the activity of all other things. For existentialism, human beings are radically alone, without God or nature to call upon when it comes to their choices. Their choices are not guided by any value or anything given. They create values when they act. Thus Jean-Paul Sartre writes, "If it is true that existence

---

it human reason, is the creation of the divine Reason, human reason would be reduced to the irrational and ultimately abolished: "[T]he issue is clearly whether or not reason stands at the beginning and foundation of all things. The issue is whether reality originates by chance and necessity, and thus whether reason is merely a chance by-product of the irrational and, in an ocean of irrationality, it too, in the end, is meaningless, or whether instead the underlying conviction of Christian faith remains true: *In principio erat Verbum*—in the beginning was the Word; at the origin of everything is the creative reason of God who decided to make himself known to us human beings" ("Meeting with the Authorities and the Diplomatic Corps"). Also see Ratzinger, "Truth of Christianity?" 181.

18. Spaemann, *Persons*, 210.

precedes essence, we can never explain our actions by reference to a given and immutable human nature. In other words, there is no determinism— man is free, man is freedom. . . . We are left alone and without excuse."[19] For him, existentialism alone takes human persons seriously, not allowing them to be exonerated from their responsibility by referring to God or nature. Rather, in every instant, with every choice and every action, human beings are effectively defining humanity for themselves.[20]

To support his point Sartre gives the example of a young Frenchman— in fact, a student of Sartre's—who found himself in the following situation during the time of the Nazi-occupation of France: his brother had been killed in the war while his father was essentially a collaborator with the occupying forces. To his mother, who was living alone with him, he was the last remaining reason to live. At the same time, he found his country invaded by the enemy and felt the need to revenge his brother. What should he do? Stay with his mother who is so much in need of his presence, or join the French resistance army in Great Britain? Sartre claims that this young man "was vacillating between two kinds of morality: a morality motivated by sympathy and individual devotion, and another morality with a broader scope, but less likely to be fruitful. He had to choose between the two."[21] For this choice, according to our French existentialist, there exist no criteria:

> What could help him make that choice? The Christian doctrine? No. The Christian doctrine tells us we must be charitable, love our neighbor, sacrifice ourselves for others, choose the "narrow way," et cetera. But what is the narrow way? . . . Which is the more useful aim—the vague one of fighting as part of a group, or the more concrete one of helping one particular person keep on living? Who can decide that *a priori*? No one.[22]

From this example Sartre concludes that we have to act from a radical choice. We are not acting according to our nature, since there is no such thing. Our choices, in other words, are as radical as is our freedom, without criteria for judgment or guidance. Our action is not measured by the good but rather creative of it: "Choosing to be this or that is to affirm at

---

19. Sartre, *Existentialism Is a Humanism*, 29.

20. See ibid.: "Existentialists . . . think . . . that man is therefore without any support or help, condemned at all times to invent man."

21. Ibid., 31.

22. Ibid.

the same time the value of what we choose."[23] Then, of course, it becomes impossible ever to choose anything bad, since the good is defined precisely as that which is chosen. Hence Sartre writes, "we can never choose evil. We always choose the good."[24] Why do we act, then? We act in order to create ourselves and our values, and along with that we reinvent humanity.

Yet, one can and must challenge the conclusions Sartre draws from his example. Is it really true that by our action we "create" values, or are our actions not guided by some criteria that precede our choices? In fact, Charles Taylor gives a very insightful response to Sartre, arguing that Sartre's example of the young man considering to join the French resistance army is actually proving the opposite of what it is intended to show. Taylor points out that the alternative proposed in Sartre's example is precisely between two highly significant options. The mere fact that one may find it hard to counsel the young man to do one thing or the other does not demonstrate that the importance of either option is created by the one who chooses. Taylor puts it this way: "Sartre's portrayal of the dilemma is very powerful. But what makes it plausible is precisely what undermines his position. We see a grievous moral dilemma because the young man is faced here with two powerful moral claims."[25] In other words, the alternative is not between staying with his needful mother on the one hand and eating an ice-cream on the other hand, for example. Taylor continues, "It is a dilemma only because the claims themselves are not created by radical choice. If they were, the grievous nature of the predicament would dissolve, for that would mean that the young man could do away with the dilemma at any moment by simply declaring one of the rival claims as dead and inoperative.... Moral dilemmas become inconceivable on the theory of radical choice."[26] Unless either option were imbued with an importance that is not of the young man's making, the young man would not so much as feel a conflict.

In other words, ideas such as "radical choice," the human being's "condemnation to freedom," and the "reinvention of humanity" beautifully express the existentialist pathos. At the same time, for it not to become ridiculous, this pathos needs to be *about* something important, an importance that is precisely not made, but found. Thus, Sartre's words have a certain power of rhetoric when he says, "if I decide to marry and have children

---

23. Ibid., 24.
24. Ibid.
25. Taylor, "What Is Human Agency?" 29.
26. Ibid., 30.

... I am ... committing not only myself, but all of humanity, to the practice of monogamy. I am therefore responsible for myself and for everyone else, and I am fashioning a certain image of man as I choose him to be."[27] The power of Sartre's words depends entirely on the fact that the decision in question is of a certain weight, a weight that is prior to the choice. In other words, it is little plausible to claim that if I decide to eat a chocolate chip cookie, I am thereby committing not only myself, but all humanity to the practice of consuming such sweets and preferring them over peanut butter cookies. In the end, it seems that the most plausible way to respond to our initial question, i.e., "Why do we act?" is that we act because we love, or, put in the more modern parlance of Harry Frankfurt: we act because we care about the things that are important to us.[28]

Why Do We Love the Things We Love?

The Truth about "The Importance of What We Care About"

Frankfurt's response, however, still leaves us somewhat puzzled, since one can of course evidently continue to ask, "Why are the things that we care about important to us?" and "Why do we love the things we love?" Here, Frankfurt observes that "it certainly cannot be assumed that what a person cares about is generally under his immediate voluntary control."[29] Things are not important to us simply because we decide to care for them. There are in fact some "principles of discrimination" that make one thing a more appropriate object of our care than another. As Frankfurt writes, "Although people may justifiably care about different things, or care differently about the same things, this surely does not mean that their loves and their ideals are entirely unsusceptible to significant criticism of any sort or that no general analytical principles of discrimination can be found."[30]

Frankfurt does not continue to specify where exactly we can find the criteria for a significant criticism of our loves, but to our mind it is difficult to see how at this point we could go on without bringing in the concept of nature. What it means to have a nature is precisely this: that there are things that are originally important to a given being, that there exist certain

---

27. Sartre, *Existentialism Is a Humanism*, 24–25.

28. See Frankfurt, *The Importance of What We Care About*.

29. Ibid., 85.

30. Ibid., 91.

goods that it cannot help caring about. Nature here is understood not as a static givenness but a proper principle of rest and motion, as a dynamic principle of development that actively seeks to actualize its potentialities. As Aristotle says, "the 'what' and 'that for the sake of which' are one,"[31] i.e., the nature is itself the end, because the aim of its striving is the full actualization of its potentialities. That which actualizes a nature is the good. Hence the good will be important to that nature. This is the case with any nature, human nature included. The question of which goods are fulfilling of a nature depends on each given nature, and these goods in turn define a given nature as what it is. While eucalyptus leaves are poisonous to most animals, they represent a koala's favorite food. They are a good for koalas but not for other animals.

Traditionally, four types of goods have been listed as defining *human* nature. These are indicated by the fundamental human inclinations and are also called the principles of the natural moral law:[32]

1. self-preservation along with physical integrity;

2. the union of the sexes and the raising of children;

3. knowledge, and particularly knowledge about God and the meaning of life;

4. life in society and friendship.[33]

These fundamental goods are the essential characteristics of human nature and for St. Thomas, whatever pertains to these goods "belongs to the natural law; for instance, to shun ignorance, to avoid offending those among whom one has to live, and other such things."[34] In his encyclical *Veritatis Splendor*, Pope John Paul II speaks of these goods as "goods for the person."[35] Along

---

31. Aristotle, *Physics*, II, 7, 198a24–27.

32. See Aquinas, *Summa Theologica*, I-II, 94, 2: "Since, however, good has the nature of an end, and evil, the nature of a contrary, hence it is that all those things to which man has a natural inclination, are naturally apprehended by reason as being good, and consequently as objects of pursuit, and their contraries as evil, and objects of avoidance. Wherefore according to the order of natural inclinations, is the order of the precepts of the natural law."

33. See ibid., I-II, 94, 2.

34. Ibid.

35. John Paul II, *Veritatis Splendor*, no. 79: "The primary and decisive element for moral judgment is the object of the human act, which establishes whether it is capable of being ordered to the good and to the ultimate end, which is God. This capability is grasped by reason in the very being of man, considered in his integral truth, and

with being the principles of precepts, these goods tell us that when we meet a human being, we meet a being for whom the questions of life, sexuality, friendship and meaning matter. These are issues that human beings naturally care about, such that no human being could simply decide that these are not important. Though Richard Dawkins is a professed atheist, he nonetheless keeps speaking about God,[36] demonstrating that the question of God matters to him by the very pains he takes in denying God's existence. Neither was Jean-Paul Sartre able, by a radical choice, to decide that God was not important, confessing that existentialists "find it extremely disturbing that God no longer exists."[37] The question of God along with the question of the meaning of life matters even to the existentialist. It is an importance that is given, not chosen. The same holds true also for issues regarding friendship, sexuality and self-preservation. When Albert Camus claims that the only significant question for philosophy is why not to commit suicide, he necessarily implies that the question of life is important.[38]

Evaluating Our Reasons

Hence we see that human freedom has criteria for its choices. If freedom meant the jump into a void, our choices would be random chance events without rhyme or reason. In this case one could no more speak of freedom as in the case of causally determined events.[39] Yet, to be free, it is not enough just to have reasons for acting because presumably animals, too, have things that are important to them.[40] What distinguishes humans from all other living beings is that humans not only have reasons for acting, but they alone

---

therefore in his natural inclinations, his motivations and his finalities, which always have a spiritual dimension as well. It is precisely these which are the contents of the natural law and hence that ordered complex of 'personal goods' [Latin: "bonorum pro persona" = "goods for the person"] which serve the 'good of the person': the good which is the person himself and his perfection."

36. See Dawkins, *The God Delusion*.

37. Sartre, *Existentialism Is a Humanism*, 28.

38. See Camus, *Myth of Sisyphus*, 3: "There is but one truly serious philosophical problem, and that is suicide."

39. See Taylor, "What Is Human Agency?" 33: "A criteria-less leap . . . can not properly be described as choice at all."

40. See MacIntyre, *Dependent Rational Animals*, 55: "The wolf and the sheep have reasons for acting as they do, even although they do not have the power of reason."

can *evaluate these reasons.*[41] Here we may be touching at the heart of what it means to be free and what it means to be a person. Harry Frankfurt speaks of "second-order volitions,"[42] while Robert Spaemann would prefer to call this phenomenon by the name of "primary will."[43] Karol Wojtyła speaks of the horizon of the truth about the good: To choose means "to make a decision, according to the principle of truth, upon selecting between possible objects that have been presented to the will. . . . The will . . . *responds* to motives instead of being in one way or another only determined by them. . . . This response presupposes a reference to *truth* and not only a reference to the *objects* which elicit it."[44] In other words, persons' independence of the objects (goods) that are presented to them means that they can let themselves be *motivated* by these objects; persons are not *caused* by the objects. Persons are independent of objects because they are dependent on truth. Wojtyła and the other authors just mentioned more or less point to the same fact: human persons can judge the very reasons for which they are acting. The criterion they use in this case is their fundamental love, their primary willing, that which they have come to regard as the truth about the good, that which they *truly* want. It is the truth about the good, or—as *Veritatis Splendor* calls it—the "good of the person,"[45] that allows them to evaluate their desires, wishes, and actions.

However, judging from the horizon of the truth about the good does not mean that people will always do the right thing; they may miss the mark.[46] What is initially being affirmed here is simply that practical

41. See ibid., 53–61. See also Taylor, "What Is Human Agency?" 15–16: "What is distinctively human is the power to *evaluate* our desires" (original emphasis).

42. Frankfurt, *Importance of What We Care About*, 16.

43. Spaemann, *Persons*, 206.

44. Wojtyła, *Acting Person*, 137–38 (original emphases). For an introduction to this complex philosophical work, see Acosta and Reimers, *Karol Wojtyła's Personalist Philosophy.*

45. See for instance, John Paul II, *Veritatis Splendor*, no. 13: "The different commandments of the Decalogue are really only so many reflections of the one commandment about the good of the person, at the level of the many different goods which characterize his identity as a spiritual and bodily being in relationship with God, with his neighbour and with the material world."

46. See Wojtyła, *Acting Person*, 139: "Let us stress once again the need to examine more precisely the 'moment of truth.' But first it is perhaps worth noting that this moment, which belongs to the will, is to be distinguished from the truthfulness of the *particular choices and decisions* that may be actually made. . . . First, there is the painfully evident fact that not all of the particular choices or decisions of the human will are correct. Too often man seeks and chooses what is not good for him" (original emphasis).

questions admit of truth and falsity. The truth about the good allows for the possibility of persons evaluating their desires, discerning the reasons for their acting. It means that, Sartre to the contrary, persons' actions will not be good by definition or good because they chose them, but that their desires as well as their actions can be evaluated. The fact that people at times reach different conclusions in their evaluations is not an argument for relativism. Thus Leo Strauss points out that the existence of what he calls "natural right," or what we may well call "the truth about the good," is the condition for the possibility of there being disagreement.[47] When people in one society pay in dollars and in another they do so in euros, we do not say that these two societies disagree with each other. Currencies are conventional and there is no absolute truth about them. We do say, however, that two societies or even two individuals are in authentic disagreement when they differ on issues such as people's right to life, their freedom of speech or religion. The very fact that they do disagree on these issues shows that here we are dealing with questions that are not simply conventional but that admit of truth and falsity.

The Calling of the Good and the Calling to Communion

Given that we do not create the good with our choices, i.e., that we have *reasons* for acting that are not of our own making, and given that we can in turn evaluate these reasons in the light of the truth about the good, how exactly does this evaluation come about? It would be a misapprehension to think that after having listed the natural human goods or inclinations we have said everything there is to be said about the teleology of human action. Human persons do not act simply *in order to* fulfill their potentialities. Speaking in this way, we would fall back again into the "inversion of teleology" we have talked about above. The fulfillment of their nature would then be the greatest good for human beings, while we had started out with the hypothesis that even the fulfillment of a nature could still be

---

47. See Strauss, *Natural Right and History,* 100: "As regards such things as are unquestionably conventional—weights, measures, money, and the like—one can hardly speak of disagreement between various societies. Different societies make different arrangements in regard to weights, measures, and money; these arrangements do not contradict one another. But if different societies hold different views regarding the principles of justice, their views contradict one another. Differences regarding things which are unquestionably conventional do not arouse serious perplexities, whereas differences regarding the principles of right and wrong necessarily do."

for the sake of something; for instance, for the sake of participating in the divine, as Aristotle said.

There is an additional problem with looking at action simply as a way of fulfilling human potentialities. It consists in the fact that what it means for a human being to fulfill his or her nature is less defined than in the case of other beings. The end of an acorn is to become an oak, and what it means to be an oak that has fulfilled its oak-nature does not allow for much diversity.[48] With human beings, on the other hand, there seem to be very different walks of life and ways of being that could possibly be said to be fulfilling of human nature. People may nurture their athletic abilities, neglecting any musical talent naturally inherent in them; some may become very good mathematicians but miserable swimmers. True excellence in one field would in fact exclude the possibility of building strong abilities in other non-related fields. Even if we take the much larger perspective of moral virtue, human beings can possibly live their lives well as kings or philosophers, as married or celibate, as rich or poor.

This variety of possible, though at times contrary, actualizations of human nature is due to the fact that persons stand in a different relation to their nature as do other living beings. Persons can relate to their nature— they *own* their nature. Spaemann puts it this way, "A nature is a principle of specific reaction. With the concept of the person, however, we come to think of the particular individual as being more basic than its nature. This is not to suggest that these individuals have no nature, and start out by deciding for themselves what they are to be. What they do is assume a new relation to their nature; they freely endorse the laws of their being, or alternatively they rebel against them and 'deviate.'"[49] Only persons, in other words, can act contrary to their nature—which does not mean that to do so is recommendable—and only for them, nature can be a criterion and guide. For a lion, its lion-nature cannot be said to *guide* the lion in its acts inasmuch as it is completely determined by its nature. The principle of its activity is its nature and its nature alone.

Furthermore, the guidance that their nature can offer to persons in their acts is mostly negative. It can identify certain acts that are never to be done, but it leaves open a vast field of creativity in the good.[50] Persons

48. See Belardinelli, *Bioetica tra natura e cultura*, 50–51.

49. Spaemann, *Persons*, 33.

50. See Melina, *Epiphany of Love*, 73: "Beyond the respect of limits, Christian morality promotes the creativity of love and the personal and unique response that each of us is called to give to the Love that has revealed itself to us."

cannot choose and pursue all the possible goods that are presented to them, but rather they must choose some, preferring some to others. This is a real drama, which Maurice Blondel expresses in these terms: "We do not go forward, we do not learn, we do not enrich ourselves except by closing off for ourselves all roads but one and by impoverishing ourselves of all that we might have known or gained otherwise. . . . Each determination cuts off an infinity of possible acts. . . . I must commit myself under pain of losing everything."[51]

Again, the capacity to choose, i.e., to prefer some goods to others, implies that human persons are in some measure independent of these goods. As we have said, they can evaluate their reasons, they can allow themselves to be motivated by their reasons, but are not caused by them. However, how do persons evaluate their reasons and how do they allow themselves to be motivated by some goods but not by others? Here we would like to suggest that the light that allows them to do so is shed by their love, love no longer understood generally as a natural desire but as *interpersonal communion*. What gives light and direction to their choices, then, is not *what* they love but *who* they love.

It is true that maintaining myself in being is naturally important to me, and it is a fact that I do many things for this purpose. Inasmuch as I want my survival and strive for it, it is correct to say that I love my own survival. And yet more has to be said.[52] Let us come back to the distinction with which we began: the distinction between in-order-to, or utility, and for-the-sake-of, or meaning. While my survival is an end towards which many of my actions are means, and while it is hence true to say that I love my own survival, it is nonetheless *not* true to say that my survival could serve as my actions' ultimate for-the-sake-of. My survival, as important as it is to me, is not the meaning of my existence. In fact, my survival reveals a new and fuller importance to me in the light of interpersonal love. It is the light of communion that provides meaning for my life. It is only in the encounter with another person that the chain of utility, the chain of means and ends, is broken up and the horizon of meaning is opened. The simple natural

---

51. Blondel, *Action*, 4.

52. That is, it has to be said that created persons, such as angels or human beings, do not naturally love themselves above all else, but naturally love God more than themselves. See Aquinas, *Summa Theologica*, I, 60, 5: "Since God is the universal good, and under this good both man and angel and all creatures are comprised, because every creature in regard to its entire being naturally belongs to God, it follows that from natural love angel and man alike love God before themselves and with a greater love."

tendency to keep myself in being takes on a fully personal significance—it appears in the light of love—when I keep myself in being for the sake of the persons who love me and for the sake of the persons I love.

In a similar way we must look at the other goods we have listed above. For human beings sexuality and all that is connected with it is a good in the sense that it is fulfilling of their nature. But people do not get married or raise their children simply *in order to* fulfill their nature. Rather, they marry *for their spouse's sake* and educate their children *for their children's sake.* The same is to be said for friendship and knowledge about God. What we aim at here is not primarily the fulfillment of our nature; rather we care about our friends for *their* sake and about God for *his* sake. It is in the context of interpersonal relationships, in the context of the communion of persons, that our actions become truly meaningful. We act because we love, but what we ultimately love are neither things nor the state of a fulfilled nature, but persons. The good of the person is realized in the communion of persons.[53] A simple example from everyday life may serve here: there is an experiential difference between cleaning one's house simply because it is time to do so, and cleaning it because one's friends are coming over. The latter is much less vexing because it is much more meaningful inasmuch as we do it for our friends' sake. It is the persons we love that provide the context of meaning for our actions. When a person's ultimate for-the-sake-of is God, we speak of charity. God, the Creator, in fact, calls us to the true good, and what is more, through Christ he calls us "to become his friend[s] and share his own divine life," as *Veritatis Splendor* puts it.[54] In fact, he calls us in every finite good that participates in his goodness, and it is our ordination to this absolute good, that is, communion with God, that allows us to be free before every finite good.[55]

It seems to be a defining characteristic of personal existence that a person can take genuine interest in someone outside of him- or herself, which is why Karol Wojtyła says that "transcendence is as if another name

53. See John Paul II, *Veritatis Splendor*, no. 86: "Freedom [as the human being's capacity for the good] then is rooted in the truth about man, and it is ultimately directed towards communion."

54. Ibid.

55. International Theological Commission, *In Search of a Universal Ethic*, no. 77: "As regards these [finite] goods, which exercise an attraction that does not determine the will, the person retains mastery of his choice by reason of an innate openness to the absolute Good."

for the person."[56] Persons are not locked in themselves, seeing everything as a function of the promotion of their own being. Rather, they are capable of what Leibniz calls "rejoicing in the happiness of another."[57] And even more: they are beings that awaken to themselves only through others.[58] "The Thou is older than the I,"[59] Friedrich Nietzsche quite wisely pointed out. It is only because others speak to me that I myself begin speaking and that I can start reflecting upon myself. I can only say "I" because someone else has first addressed me as "you."

If it is true that persons first come to themselves in the encounter with other persons, then it is also feasible to conclude that it is in the encounter, in the context of interpersonal communion, that they find their true fulfillment,[60] which in a certain way transcends the fulfillment of their nature, which is the case, for instance, when a man gives his life for his friends. Of such a one the Holy Scripture attests the greatest love (see John 15:13). And yet, enduring death is certainly not "fulfilling" of nature, seen from a merely naturalistic point of view. At the same time, however, giving one's life for one's friends is such a significant act precisely because life is such a great good. We see that accomplishing the good of the person does not mean simply fulfilling all the potentialities of human nature but rather realizing the meaning of one's existence, for which nature, however, remains a criterion.[61] This meaning is defined in the context of interpersonal

56. Wojtyła, "Person: Subject and Community," 230.

57. Leibniz, *Codex Iuris Gentium*, 171.

58. See Spaemann, *Persons*, 216: "A person 'has' a nature, but that nature is not what the person *is*, because the person has the power to relate freely to it. But the person cannot do so on his or her own but only through the encounter with other persons. Only the affirmation of other centres of existence—as recognition, justice, and love—allows us the distance on ourselves and the appropriation of ourselves that is constitutive for persons—in sum, 'freedom from self'" (translation slightly modified in view of the original German, original emphasis).

59. Nietzsche, *Thus Spoke Zarathustra*, 53.

60. See Pérez-Soba, "La famiglia, prima fonte," 62–63: "If the human person is awakened to his freedom and self-awareness in the encounter with others, an encounter that necessarily needs to be called *love*, then we can conclude that the perfect good of man can be understood only as the specific union of love that is established with other persons, that is, the *good of communion among persons*" (my own translation, original emphases).

61. Ibid., 53: "The relation that is established between nature and the personal calling is, first and foremost, a question of *meaning*" (my own translation, original emphasis).

communion with God and all the friends of God: it is the fulfillment of a vocation, the vocation to love.[62]

The realization of this meaning is not completely detached from the goods for the person, the fundamental "importances" of human nature. It is the truth of these that offers the criterion for whether or not a certain act is truly an act of love towards one's friends.[63] I cannot violate a very important good for the person—such as directly take his or her life—and then claim that it was an act of love. Thus murder is not evil simply because it violates a natural tendency but because it violates human dignity, as such destroying the communion among human beings.[64] And yet again, it only violates human dignity and destroys communion because it is about a matter of natural importance for human beings: their very life. *Veritatis Splendor* speaks from this personalistic perspective when it says that acts in conformity with the "common law" "build up the true communion of persons" while acts that violate the law "damage the communion of persons, to the detriment of each."[65] Thus, the natural law does not simply move from a reading of the human person's natural tendencies to precepts about right and wrong, while at the same time, it is not independent of these either. It reads the human beings' fundamental natural "importances" in the light of love, i.e., in the light of interpersonal communion. The communion among

62. See Melina, Noriega, and Pérez-Soba, *Camminare nella luce*, 630: "Still prior to being a characteristic of Christian experience, the vocation needs to be recognized as a structure of human existence as such. . . . Human freedom is in fact always provoked and called upon by reality, upon which it hits and which urges it to action. Reality, especially the reality that has the personal face of encounters, bonds, and relationships, always has the character of an event that takes place and that calls the person on, asking for a decision" (my own translation). On the topic of the vocation to love, particularly as developed by John Paul II, see also Anderson and Granados, *Called to Love*.

63. See Melina, *Epiphany of Love*, 38: "The good of a particular action, which our will chooses from the perspective of communion, has an objective weight, independent of the subject, which must be verified by reason as to its capacity to effectively promote the good of the person of the other. . . . The good's objectivity, recognized in an original way by reason, is the condition of authenticity for the communion that is sought after and that is dependent on what precedes the intention."

64. See John Paul II, *Veritatis Splendor*, no. 50: "The origin and the foundation of the duty of absolute respect for human life are to be found in the dignity proper to the person and not simply in the natural inclination to preserve one's own physical life."

65. See ibid., no. 51: "By submitting to the common law, our acts build up the true communion of persons and, by God's grace, practise charity, 'which binds everything together in perfect harmony' (*Col* 3:14). When on the contrary they disregard the law, or even are merely ignorant of it, whether culpably or not, our acts damage the communion of persons, to the detriment of each."

human beings and between human beings and God is the light in which to read our natural inclinations.[66] It is in the light of love that nature becomes a criterion for acting, the communion of love providing the ultimate for-the-sake-of of all we do. Why do we act? It is love that gives us the reasons for acting, reasons which in turn we can evaluate in the light of the communion among human beings.

---

66. See for instance Melina, "Pragmatic and Christological Foundations," 302: "The filial, fraternal, and spousal body of Christ is thus the foundation of the obedience, fraternal love, and self-giving that are at the heart of the Christian moral life. The horizon of love, which is revealed in the Eucharist, is the definitive hermeneutic for those meanings that are always already anticipated by man's natural inclinations and which are inscribed by the Creator in the human body."

4

Intercultural Dialogue and God's
Project for the Family

Dogma, Culture, and History

Cultural Diversity and the Historicity
of Human Existence

It is well known that, in very rare cases, family bonds cannot be
claimed to exist. A telling example comes from the Nayar, a very
large group living on the Malabar coast of India. In former times,
the warlike type of life of the Nayar men did not allow them to
found a family. Marriage was a purely symbolical ceremony which
did not result in a permanent tie between a man and a woman. As
a matter of fact, married women were permitted to have as many
lovers as they wished.[1]

T HIS IS AN EXAMPLE cultural anthropologist Claude Lévi-Strauss adduces
to contradict what he calls the extreme position held by a number of
his colleagues, namely the idea that "the family, consisting of a more or less
durable union, socially approved, of a man, a woman, and their children, is
a universal phenomenon, present in each and every type of society."[2] In his

---

1. Lévi-Strauss, "The Family," 334–35.

2. Ibid., 334.

essay he presents cases of socially sanctioned polygamy and polyandry,[3] of group marriages[4] and even of instances in which highly ranked women are allowed to marry other women.[5] For him, this is proof that monogamy is not inscribed in human nature.[6] As is well known, for him the *one* universal cultural norm governing marriage is the incest taboo,[7] which, however, is still subject to divergent interpretations. Thus, certain groups distinguish between different types of cousins, and while making the same distinctions, these tribes come to opposite conclusions: for one group a certain kind of cousin makes a preferable spouse, while for the other tribe marrying the same kind of cousin constitutes a sin to which death would be preferable.[8]

Given this great cultural variety, what sense does it make for the church to claim that monogamous and indissoluble marriage between a man and a woman appertains to the natural law? What meaning could any appeal to a truth about the human being have in a world of cultural diversity? Isn't the insistence on the Christian ideal of marriage as the basis of the family a kind of cultural colonialism that imposes one particular way of living on other peoples and cultures? Do not all the different forms of living together that are described by Lévi-Strauss in their particular contexts have a certain justification and reasonableness, expressing something valid about the ultimately incomprehensible mystery that is the human person? In an essay written at the turn of the millennium, Cardinal Joseph Ratzinger formulates the issue in these terms:

3. See ibid., 336–37.

4. See ibid., 338.

5. See ibid., 345–46: "In several parts of Africa, women of high rank were allowed to marry other women and have them bear children through the services of unacknowledged male lovers, the noble woman being then entitled to become the 'father' of her children and to transmit to them, according to the prevalent father's right, her own name, status and wealth."

6. See ibid., 340: "That monogamy is not inscribed in the nature of man is sufficiently evidenced by the fact that polygamy exists in widely different forms and in many types of societies."

7. See ibid., 350: "It will never be sufficiently emphasized that, if social organization had a beginning, this could only have consisted in the incest prohibition since, as we have just shown, the incest prohibition is, in fact, a kind of remodeling of the biological conditions of mating and procreation . . . compelling them to become perpetuated, only in an artificial framework of taboos and obligations. It is there, and only there, that we find a passage from nature to culture, from animal to human life."

8. See ibid., 353.

Christianity's claim to universality, which is based on the universality of truth, is often countered in our day with the argument of the relativity of cultures. It is maintained that, in fact, the Christian missionary effort did not disseminate a truth which is the same for all people, but instead subjugated indigenous cultures to the particular culture of Europe, thus damaging the richness of those cultures that had evolved among a variety of peoples.

The Christian missionary effort thus appears as another of the great European sins, as the original form of colonialism and thus as the spiritual despoiling of other peoples.[9]

On top of this, to ask about culture is also to ask about history. As Ratzinger puts it elsewhere: "Society marches onward, and therefore culture also has to do with history. On its journey through time, culture develops through its encounter with new reality and the arrival of new insights."[10] Cultures are open to meet and to progress. Particularly "the Judaeo-Christian cultural world . . . understands the way with God as history. History is thus fundamental to it."[11] Historical existence means existence in time, which is an insight that has been very much emphasized by contemporary philosophy. Thus, for Martin Heidegger temporality is at the core not only of human culture but of human existence as such: "The being of Da-sein finds its meaning in temporality. But temporality is at the same time the condition of the possibility of historicity."[12]

The question of course arises where this and other similar reflections on human temporality and historicity leave us with respect to human nature. Some see in the fact that the person's existence is temporal and historical sufficient grounds for denying human nature altogether. For José Ortega y Gasset, for instance, the whole point of history is to replace nature: "*Man, in a word, has no nature: what he has is . . . history.* Expressed differently: what nature is to things, history, *res gestae*, is to man."[13] If that is so, it will hardly be possible to define immutable dogmas and norms, inasmuch as they are meant to apply to the way of life of an essentially temporal being that is continually changing. Isn't the working document of the 2015 Synod of Bishops right when it appeals to the church's need of a *twofold* fidelity, both to "the signs of God and to human

9. Ratzinger, "Culture and Truth," 369.

10. Ratzinger, "Christ, Faith," 5.

11. Ibid.

12. Heidegger, *Being and Time*, 17 (§ 6).

13. Ortega y Gasset, *History as a System*, 217 (original emphasis and ellipses).

history"?[14] Is it not reasonable to assume that the universal law of love that Jesus taught finds different expressions and concrete applications in different historical and cultural contexts?

Cultural diversity, in any case, is a fact that needs to be reckoned with.[15] No doubt, in some cultures it is expected that men and women shake hands, while in others that is contrary to proper etiquette. There are cultures in which any public display of affection—including a couple holding hands—is considered scandalous, while in others, holding hands or a fleeting good-bye kiss are looked upon as completely acceptable. As Maurice Merleau-Ponty points out, cultural differences go extremely deep, even down to the way we not only express, but *have* emotions: "The behavior associated with anger or love is not the same in a Japanese and an Occidental. Or, to be more precise, the difference of behavior corresponds to a difference in the emotions themselves. It is not only the gesture which is contingent in relation to the body's organization, it is the manner itself in which we meet the situation and live it. The angry Japanese smiles, the westerner goes red and stamps his foot or else goes pale and hisses his words."[16]

"Inculturation"—The Faith as Formal Principle of Material Culture?

Given the great cultural diversity that is found among human beings, what is the role of the gospel? What is the relationship between the Christian faith and human cultures? In this context it has become customary to speak about "inculturation," which suggests that the faith is inserted into cultures as an immaterial form gives shape to matter. Ratzinger proposes that some indeed look at the question in this way: "One might think that the culture is the affair of the individual historical country . . . while faith for its part is in search of cultural expression. The individual cultures would allocate, as it were, a body to faith. Accordingly, faith would always have to live from

14. See Secretariat of the Synod of Bishops, *Instrumentum laboris: The Vocation and Mission of the Family*, no. 3: "The task at hand [is]: to read both the signs of God and human history, in a twofold yet unique faithfulness which this reading involves."

15. See Francis, "Concluding Address of the Fourteenth Ordinary General Assembly of the Synod of Bishops": "What seems normal for a bishop on one continent, is considered strange and almost scandalous—almost!—for a bishop from another; what is considered a violation of a right in one society is an evident and inviolable rule in another; what for some is freedom of conscience is for others simply confusion."

16. Merleau-Ponty, *Phenomenology of Perception*, 219.

borrowed cultures which remain in the end somehow external and capable of being cast off. Above all, one borrowed cultural form would not speak to someone who lives in another culture."[17] It is then thinkable that there could be cultures, all informed by the gospel, that nonetheless have very different mores, depending on which "material" culture had initially lent the body to a merely formal faith. Contraception, abortion, adultery, murder, stealing and lying could be grave sins in one culture informed by the faith, while in another culture, informed by the same faith, all or some of these could be considered tolerable or even virtuous. Faith would then be allocated only on the formal level of the transcendental intention. It tells us that God's plan for human persons is to love each other. It does *not* tell us what the loving thing to do actually is. This depends on the cultural context and may vary greatly. For this approach, in one culture the deliberate killing of an innocent victim may under given circumstances be quite in accord with the love that God commands, while in another culture it may not be.

And it is true that the church has indeed interpreted a certain number of norms contained in Scripture in more or less this way: that women should cover their head when praying (1 Cor 11:5) and be silent in church (1 Cor 14:34), for instance, is usually interpreted as a rule conditioned by the cultural context of ancient Palestinian or Greco-Roman society, which has lost its binding force for other times and places. The formal level of the norm expressed in St. Paul's indications would simply seem to be: when assembling in church, women, and presumably men, too, should always act in a decorous way. It will have to be granted that what it means concretely to act decorously will vary—at times significantly—from culture to culture. Now no one has ever claimed that a woman covering her head is a moral question pertaining to the natural moral law as expressed in the Ten Commandments, and what St. Paul had in mind when he exhorted women to be silent in church is not an easy exegetical question at all. Evidently he allowed for women to pray publically and even to prophesize (these are precisely the occasions he thinks they should cover their head). Indeed, maybe all he meant was that they should not be chatting during the liturgy.

For cultural relativists, however, *all* norms, rules or laws expressed in Scripture and taught by the church—including the Ten Commandments—can and must be interpreted in the light of the cultural context in which they were first expressed. Then they would need to be translated into a different context. While moral norms tend to promote people's good,

17. Ratzinger, "Christ, Faith," 6.

one cannot discern what this good actually is without looking at the given historical and cultural contexts. On these terms, the rule of faith would always have to be incarnated ever again into different cultures. The gospel way of life will differ from country to country and from century to century. What was valid there and then is not valid here and now; what is binding on us in Europe today was not necessarily binding in Asia two centuries ago. In the words of Joseph Ratzinger: "Universality would thereby finally become fictitious."[18] The local episcopal conferences should then decide about moral issues just as they decide about which feast days should be counted among the holidays of obligation.

Let us apply this kind of thinking to the norm "Do not commit adultery," which is proposed by the Jewish-Christian faith. For ancient Jewish culture, this norm was compatible with polygamy, divorce and remarriage, while for Christian culture it was not. Evidently there has been a development here toward a stricter reading of the commandment, though according to the words of Jesus himself, his way of explaining the commandment is not the newer but the older one, corresponding to its original sense: "From the beginning it was not so" (Matt 19:8). Jesus thus did not practice any cultural hermeneutics but referred to the original plan of God, from which the culture in which he lived had deviated. However, once we get caught in what Ratzinger calls a "hall of mirrors of interpretations,"[19] we will of course interpret the evangelist's account itself as culturally conditioned. Relating given norms to the truth of God's original plan with humankind will then just be one culturally conditioned way in which people of a particular place and time tended to interpret moral norms. Thus we will be back to where we've started.

Given human beings' cultural, temporal and historical existence, who says that an exclusive and indissoluble marital relationship is really the best for them in all contexts, times and places? According to cultural relativists, to interpret "Do not commit adultery" in the sense of "Do not have non-marital relations" might have made sense in other times; it still might make sense in *some* cultures today, but it will probably have different implications in the West. In any case, on the categorical level of concrete application, it will mean something different in each cultural and historical context. Only

18. Ibid.

19. See Ratzinger, "Culture and Truth," 368: "Man is not trapped in a hall of mirrors of interpretations; one can and must seek a breakthrough to what is really true. Man must ask who he really is and what he is to do. He must ask whether there is a God, who God is, and what the world is."

on the formal level, i.e., on the level of the general intention of doing good, "Do not commit adultery" will have a universal significance. It will simply denote something like, "Treat your sexual partner fairly," but what that means concretely will always vary. Given the relatively recent acquisitions of ready access to contraception and abortion or the new understanding of the role of women in society, treating one's sexual partner fairly in the West of the twenty-first century is perhaps quite compatible with pre- and extramarital relationships or may even require them. Isn't it irresponsible, and hence unloving, to marry someone one hasn't tried out? If Robert really loves his wife Jane, should he not occasionally try out other women and also allow her to try out other men so as to give a new boost to their relationship? After all, some sociologists suggest that open relationships are often experienced as more satisfying than exclusive ones.[20]

For Ratzinger, a view that implies a dualism between faith and culture "is at root Manichean. Culture is debased, becoming a mere exchangeable shell. Faith is reduced to disincarnated spirit ultimately void of reality."[21] It is true that Christians also always belong to the cultural context of their nation. It is also the case, however, that faith itself is a culture and creates and informs a culture. The people of God is itself a cultural subject, though "as a Christian, one remains a Frenchman, a German, an American, an Indian, etc."[22] The fact is that with Christianity a "doubling of cultures" arises, "such that man now lives in two cultural worlds, his historic culture and in the new one of faith, both of which permeate him."[23] However, to say that there are two interacting cultures that mutually permeate each other—the culture of the church as the people of God and any given historical culture—is quite different from saying that "faith would always have to live from borrowed cultures,"[24] which, again, would be a Manichean approach that sees the faith as something abstract and disincarnate. The culture of faith can stand in a fruitful tension with the historical cultures that it meets for the first time. It can profit from them and deepen its insights and renew its

---

20. See Giddens, *Transformation of Intimacy*, 147: "Episodic sexuality may usually be a way of avoiding intimacy, but it also offers a means of furthering or elaborating upon it. For sexual exclusiveness is only one way in which commitment to another is protected and integrity achieved."

21. Ratzinger, "Christ, Faith," 6.

22. Ibid.

23. Ibid.

24. Ibid.

expressions. It can cleanse and heal the areas where they do not completely correspond to the truth of our humanity. As Ratzinger puts it:

> When the faith and its culture meet another culture hitherto foreign to it, it cannot be a question of dissolving the duality of the cultures to the advantage of the one or the other. Gaining a Christianity deprived of its concrete human complexion at the cost of losing one's own cultural heritage would be as mistaken as surrendering faith's own cultural physiognomy. Indeed the tension is fruitful; it renews faith and heals culture. It would therefore be nonsensical to offer a sort of pre-cultural or de-cultured Christianity which would rob itself of its own historical force and degrade itself to an empty collection of ideas.[25]

Thus the gospel is not an a-cultural reality that takes flesh in a culture only in a second moment. Rather, the gospel creates culture; it is the source of culture. The Christian vision of marriage and family is a particularly good example for the workings of what Ratzinger prefers to call "inter-culturality" rather than inculturation.[26] Marriage is a reality of the created order and can virtually be witnessed in any known cultural context.[27] It is the culture of faith that brings this reality to its fullness, strengthening what is good and pruning away what is imperfect. As the gospel is the source of culture that has repercussions, for instance, on the way people live marriage and family, so does the family itself, we may say, generate culture. The family guards the person's origin; it transmits language, symbols and narrations. If culture is indeed "the historically developed common form of expression of the insights and values which characterize the life of a community,"[28] then it is evident that the crisis of the family will be tantamount to a crisis of culture.

---

25. Ibid.

26. See ibid.: "We should no longer speak of inculturation but of the meeting of cultures or 'inter-culturality,' to coin a new phrase. For inculturation presumes that a faith stripped of culture is transplanted into a religiously indifferent culture whereby two subjects, formally unknown to each other, meet and fuse. But such a notion is first of all artificial and unrealistic, for with the exception of modern technological civilization, there is no such thing as faith devoid of culture or culture devoid of faith."

27. See Lévi-Strauss, "The Family," 340. All the cultural differences that he observed notwithstanding, Lévi-Strauss testifies that "every society has some way to operate a distinction between free unions and legitimate ones."

28. Ratzinger, "Christ, Faith," 5.

Social customs, arrangements and approaches as they are prevalent in post-modern societies, which deconstruct traditions, values, and people's bond with the past are at once anti-cultural and anti-family. At the same time, this postmodern "culture" claims its own universality. It makes the universal claim that there are no universals; it claims as immutable truth that there is no truth. It spreads from the Western to Eastern and African cultures. Its gospel proclaims that human persons are autonomous and independent. Just as they can dare know for themselves, they can live by themselves, which inevitably leads to isolation and alienation. People do not only live alone, they also die alone. It is not unusual to read in the papers about people found dead in their houses months after they had died. No one had missed them. Is this really a cultural achievement? Can one really not say anything about this? If instead we are convinced that cultures can and must be judged, then what would be a better criterion for evaluating them than looking at how they treat the root of culture, that is, marriage and the family?

Human Nature and Human Culture

The proposal of a complete relativity of cultures without any reference to human nature is not at all plausible. To claim that there is a human nature is to claim that something true can be said about the meaning of human existence and behavior, something that has universal validity throughout all times and places. On what grounds can one claim the existence of a human nature? Insofar as this discussion is going on also within the church, among theologians and bishops, it is important to remember what is at stake here theologically speaking. Evidently, Christ can be the redeemer of humankind only if there actually *is* a humankind. "The Word became flesh" (John 1:14). By assuming our nature, he elevated it and made us "partakers of the divine nature" (2 Pet 1:4). All this is possible only if there is an "us," i.e., only if it actually makes sense to speak of humans and humanity. On the nominalist position that denies human nature, there is no humanity that could be saved and elevated. There are as many modes of being as there are individuals who at most have a certain resemblance. If we deny human nature, we deny that there is a common humanity and with that we negate one of the basic conditions for redemption.

Apart from the theological implications, there are grave political ones as well. Without a common human nature, a common humanity, there is no humankind. Now the denial of our common humanity is of course the necessary premise of racism if not its very definition.

Beside the theological and political necessity of positing it, what else speaks in favor of a universal human nature common to all called by the name of human, independent of place, time and culture? There is for one the marvelous fact that, all the justified concerns of modern hermeneutics notwithstanding, we do tend to be able to understand ancient texts. Quite remarkably, scriptwriters of the Hollywood of the twentieth and twenty-first century keep using a 2300 year old manual for successful and appealing story-telling: Aristotle's *Poetics* is one of their key references.[29] Who decided that Aristotle's ideas are still relevant today? Is this simply an arbitrary choice or the result of bribery from the part of the Greek ministry of culture? No, the Philosopher's relevance simply derives from the fact that he was able to say something *true* about writing a story, something that corresponds to who we are and how we work as human beings. Martians may or may not compose a story differently. Humans of all ages, in any case, have been finding Aristotle's remarks on story-telling to be quite to the point.

Similarly, when we read historical accounts, we can generally empathize with the actors' hopes and motivations, their doubts and struggles. Despite centuries or millennia that separate us from them and the texts that describe their actions, we recognize our own humanity in them: we would be frightened by the same threats that they were afraid of; we would be appalled by the same things that outraged them; we would be attracted by the same goods they were drawn to. It is true, today we wage battles differently than in ancient times, but the reasons why we fight are essentially the same. We use different tools to till the ground and dress in different types of clothes than people did in the Middle Ages; yet we still work the field and care about the way we dress. All this would not be possible if human nature were completely transient or inexistent. Indeed, as Francesco Botturi puts it, "It is clear that, if one starts with the presupposition that human nature means *univocity of behavior*—as Montaigne thought—then the result of the research will be negative; if, instead, nature is rather understood as a *tendency that is fundamentally structured*, then the variety of forms regarding the identical interest and the same care, instead of being an objection, can be its most reasonable indirect documentation."[30]

29. See Hiltunen, *Aristotle in Hollywood*.

30. Botturi, *La generazione del bene*, 326 (my own translation; original emphases).

Perhaps even more importantly, without a human nature there could not be any human culture in the first place. As Robert Spaemann points out, "The word 'culture' comes originally from agriculture; culture is nature humanized, not abrogated."[31] The farmer is first of all confronted with a given: the field and the seed. Cultivating these means to create the best conditions to make the crops flourish and yield abundant fruit. And while nature needs culture to be brought to its fullness, it is evident that without nature culture would not have anything to cultivate. Once a field and seeds are at hand, the cultivating activity must respect their particular way of being. One can use different ways of proceeding: one can do intensive or extensive farming; one can use a tractor or a horse to pull the plow; then there are different types of fertilizers. All the while farmers have to respect the nature of the field and the nature of the seed. Different types of ground need different forms of tilling; different seeds need different fertilizers and different amounts of water. Certain ways of cultivating a field yield better results than others.

Analogously, the different human cultures are the different ways of making human nature thrive. Some make human nature thrive more than others; some may even contain elements that impede such thriving, although if a culture were completely against human nature, it would simply self-destruct and no longer be transmitted to future generations. It would become an "anti-culture." All of us live within a culture, as it is part of our nature to be cultivated. According to St. John Paul II, human culture is "that through which man as man, becomes more man, 'is' more, has more access to 'being.'"[32] Culture brings nature to its fullness. It is "characteristic of human life as such. Man lives a really human life thanks to culture."[33] For instance, human beings do not just feed; they eat and they dine. As Spaemann puts it, "Eating and drinking, as free actions . . . enter into a cultural context. They are cultivated, culturally remade. In many cultures the cooking of meals is, as Claude Lévi-Strauss has shown, the basic paradigm of culture itself. Eating and drinking become the meal, the family meal the meal with friends, the marriage banquet. In religion it becomes a sacrament, and even eternal life is presented by the image of the heavenly marriage banquet."[34] We may also think of the reality of language, which

31. Spaemann, *Happiness and Benevolence*, 167.

32. John Paul II, "Address to UNESCO," no. 7.

33. Ibid., no. 6.

34. Spaemann, *Happiness and Benevolence*, 166.

is both among the clearest expressions of *culture* and a defining element of human *nature*, contradistinguished by its capacity for the word.[35]

Furthermore, intercultural dialogue would be impossible if there were no common human nature. What we said about understanding other human beings throughout the ages is also true about understanding human beings of other cultures. How is it possible that Lévi-Strauss was able to communicate with the tribes he visited? He could dialogue with them only because he was either able to learn their language or find someone who was able to speak both theirs and his. Languages can be translated. People's reasoning can be understood, even if they are from cultures very different from our own. If there were no common nature, people from one culture could not empathize with people from another; they could not understand each other. There would not be enough common ground to be able to begin a dialogue. Cultures would just be closed off. Botturi puts it this way: "It is undeniable that, without some meta-relative reference, relativity degenerates into particularism and into incommunicability: the total relativization of differences leads to axiological in-difference and the closure of subjects and cultures."[36]

Indeed, cultural diversity is not as such an argument for the non-existence of a human nature, which of course needs to be understood in an adequate way. In fact, for Botturi, so long as we do not erroneously identify nature "with a prefixed model of behavior or with a rigid and fixed frame," the evidence gathered by cultural anthropology actually speaks in favor of its existence, inasmuch as cultural anthropology "everywhere documents the efforts to regulate sexual, familial and social relations and in general the search for the practical ordering of human generation."[37] Indeed some of the strangest customs Lévi-Strauss relates to us are not based on fundamentally different concerns—as if the people he observed belonged to a different species, unconcerned about "the practical ordering of human generation"—but depend on some very elemental speculative deficiencies. If the members of a given culture are gravely mistaken about where babies come from, not attributing to the male any role in the matter, then it is not surprising that in their culture they will regulate the male-female

---

35. See Aristotle, *Politics*, I, 1, 1253a10.

36. Botturi, *La generazione del bene*, 337 (my own translation).

37. Ibid., 325 (my own translation).

relationship in a way that is very different from how they would if they were better initiated into the biological mysteries of sexuality.[38]

Cultures are open to learning from each other, as they are all essentially about the same thing, namely about making humans flourish.[39] As Lévi-Strauss points out, their interaction is the most common phenomenon: "It is thus clear that the concept of the diversity of human cultures cannot be static. It is not the diversity of a collection of lifeless samples or the diversity to be found in the arid pages of a catalogue. . . . This would be strictly and absolutely true only if every culture or society had been born and had developed without the slightest contact with any others. Such a case never occurs however. . . . Human societies are never alone."[40] Cultures can encounter each other and interact only because they have something in common. As Ratzinger puts it, they can meet "because man, despite all the differences of his history and social constructs, remains one and the same being."[41] Just as individuals are open for each other, so are cultures. This openness "can only be explained by the hidden fact that our souls have been touched by truth, and this explains the essential agreement which exists even between cultures most removed from each other."[42] Indeed, if we look at the sapiential and legal writings of the great cultures of the most different times and places, much more striking than their diversity is the fundamental concurrence with which they recommend or oppose certain types of behavior.[43]

38. Commenting on an Australian tribe, Lévi-Strauss writes: "And since that attitude toward sexual access to a woman existed along with the official dogma that men have no part in physiological procreation (therefore doubly denying any kind of bond between the husband and his wife's children), the family becomes an economic grouping where man brings the products of his hunt and the woman those of her collecting and gathering." This major mistake regarding the question of where babies come from will necessarily have serious repercussions on the ordering of sexual behavior. Lévi-Strauss, "The Family," 336.

39. As Ratzinger puts it: "Cultures, the expression of man's one essence, are characterized by the human dynamic, which is to transcend all boundaries. Thus, cultures are not fixed once and for all in a single form; they have the capacity to make progress and to be transformed, as they also face the danger of decadence. Cultures are predisposed to the experience of encounter and reciprocal enrichment" ("Culture and Truth," 370).

40. Lévi-Strauss, *Race and History*, 9–10.

41. Ratzinger, "Christ, Faith," 6.

42. Ibid.

43. A highly instructive list of sapiential recommendations, legal norms and moral precepts stemming from a great diversity of cultures—such as, for instance, ancient Babylonian, Egyptian, Chinese, Hindu, Greek and Roman cultures—is adduced in the appendix of C.S. Lewis's outstanding booklet *The Abolition of Man*, 95–121.

Cultural Relativism and the Common Truth

Among today's cultural relativists inside and outside the church, among those who consider the faith an essentially cultureless phenomenon that needs to be inculturated into different contexts, one notices a curious fact. Most of their relativism is limited to questions pertaining to the sixth commandment. One needs to remember, though, that the commandments are ten in number. One may at least wonder whether advocates of cultural relativism would as readily apply to the fifth or seventh commandment the cultural hermeneutic they use for the sixth.[44] One will hope, at least, that they will not. Otherwise, what would they say about the ritual murder practiced among the Aztecs and the infanticide that was common among the Spartans? Could these "cultural" practices ever be consistent with the faith? Do these practices give witness to the fact that the commandment "Do not kill" does not express any universal truth about human nature, that it always needs to be interpreted within a given culture, and that it has to be concretely applied according to the context of the times? All this cultural relativists would have to affirm to be consistent in the logic that they apply to the sixth commandment whereby they conclude from the fact that some cultures practice polygamy or wife-lending to the affirmation that the sixth commandment is not universally binding or takes on different and even contrary meanings, depending on the context. But do the "cultural" practices of the Aztecs and Spartans not rather give evidence to the fact that cultures can and must indeed be judged by the measure of a truth that is potentially common to all but that can at times become obscured; that historical cultures can be severely wounded and fail to make human nature flourish, thus standing in need of the healing power of the gospel culture?[45] This is the position that has been advocated in this chapter.

Incidentally, those who claim that there is a truth about the human person do not thereby assert that they hold or possess this truth and now

44. Taking the case of the murderers of the Third Reich, John Lawrence Hill points out that "if the cultural relativist were right, all we could do about the Nazis was say that we disagree with them and then punish them for the actions we found abhorrent once we had the power to do so. But the consistent cultural relativist must admit that we had no rational ground for our disapproval and no moral ground for finding the Nazis guilty of 'crimes against humanity'" (*After the Natural Law*, 236).

45. In the case at hand, the confrontation with any other culture that deserves this name and that does not consider the slaughtering of human beings a practice pleasing to the gods could have potentially helped the Aztecs to become more human and humane, to overcome what are really their *anti*-cultural practices.

intend to impose it on everyone else who is not thus enlightened. Even on the most superficial inspection, it is quite evident that the affirmation, "The question of the human person admits of a truth; there is a good and a bad for human beings; they can flourish and they can perish" is not quite the same as the declaration, "I possess the truth about the human person; the way I say is good for human beings; if they do otherwise, they will perish." If there is no truth, then there will be nothing that is common, and there will be no ground for dialogue or reasoning. Hence it is precisely those who *negate* the truth—and not those who affirm it—who will have to *impose* their views on others (as long, in any case, as they desire to share them with others). Without truth, arguments have no basis, and "sharing" one's views inevitably becomes a battle of will and power. Truth is what is common. No human being possesses it, though we can all share in it to greater and lesser degrees. Dialogue, conversation, philosophical argument: all these are ways in which we help each other to participate ever more deeply in the common truth.

At times, indeed, in our heart of hearts, we know much more of this common truth than we want to admit, also because acknowledging this truth may require us to change our ways. How come, for instance, it is so difficult for people of Western cultures to see that the human embryo is a human being with all the substantial capacities that define human nature? How come it is so difficult to derive practical conclusions from this fact, even if it is acknowledged? Doing so would require a fundamentally different way of relating to human procreation. People in Western societies would have to change profoundly the way they engage in sexual activity. Though as such called for by reality, such change is difficult and costly. Here is how a historical culture can blind itself. It ever needs to be confronted with the culture of the gospel that brings the light of God's revelation to moments in history where the human intellect is obscured and blinded even to the most obvious facts, which on principle human beings could know quite well even with their unaided reason. Faith indeed generates culture, calling us to conversion and reminding us of God's original plan for the human person, for marriage, and for the family.

PART TWO

Society and Utopia

Befriending Our Limits

5

A Promise to Keep: Which Bond, Whose Fidelity?

Introduction

"**O**NE OUGHT NOT TO understand this teaching [of the indissoluble bond] as a kind of metaphysical hypostasis beside or over the personal love of the spouses."[1] These are the words pronounced by Cardinal Walter Kasper before the Extraordinary Consistory in February 2014 with which he warns against thinking of the marital bond as having an ontological status of its own apart from the love of the people who are bound by it. For him, attributing too much metaphysical weight to the bond may confuse the debate on the question of granting some form of ecclesial recognition to those living in a second union while their spouse is still alive.[2]

Now the bond, whatever its ontological status may be, is created by the spouses' marital promises. If we want to understand what kind of consistency is proper to the bond, we should begin with a discussion of what is involved in promising in general and then, more in particular, in promising marital fidelity. In what follows, we will begin by looking at the thought of some highly influential philosophers on the matter, hoping to learn from

---

1. Kasper, *Gospel of the Family*, 16. For an in-depth analysis and critique of Kasper's position in general, see Pérez-Soba and Kampowski, *The Gospel of the Family*.

2. This is, all of Kasper's protestations notwithstanding, the main issue of the Cardinal's speech and of the subsequent booklet in which the speech was published together with some added material.

them, but also wishing to see the roots of some extremely significant conceptual errors on the matter that are prone to obscure the question of the nature of the marital bond. In due course we will ask the following questions: What is a promise? Does a promise oblige and if yes, why? Why do we promise? To whom or what do we pledge fidelity when we promise? What is specific to the marital promise?

The Promise as a Social Convention
in Hume and Hobbes

For David Hume making a promise and being faithful to it is not a "natural virtue."[3] The word "natural" here will have to be understood in its contrast to "social" or "conventional." Indeed, *a promise wou'd not be intelligible, before human conventions had established it; and . . . even if it were intelligible, it wou'd not be attended with any moral obligation.*[4] The institution of promising exists in a given society because, undoubtedly, promises are useful and advantageous. Hume gives the example of organizing an imminent harvest. If my crops are ripe today and yours will be tomorrow and if none of us has enough capacity to harvest by ourselves, then I would ask you to help me today and promise you that I will help you tomorrow.[5] Given that in Hume's anthropology human beings are essentially egoistic, there is little hope you would help me just out of fellow-feeling: "Men being naturally selfish, or endow'd only with a confin'd generosity, they are not easily induced to perform any action for the interest of strangers, except with a view to some reciprocal advantage, which they had no hope of obtaining but by such a performance."[6] You will only help me today if you can rest assured that I will help you tomorrow. Without the institution of promising, you will not help me, nor will I help you, and both of us will lose our harvests.[7]

We see clearly that it is useful to promise. According to this account, *the purpose of the institution of promising is to make people do what we want them to do without having to use force or deceit.* It is a function of

3. Hume, *Treatise of Human Nature*, 333: "There is naturally no inclination to observe promises, distinct from a sense of their obligation; it follows, that fidelity is no natural virtue, and that promises have no force, antecedent to human conventions."

4. Ibid., 331 (original emphasis).

5. See ibid., 334.

6. Ibid., 333.

7. Ibid., 334.

the interested commerce of humankind, which is also why, for Hume, we do not promise to people who are close to us, but only to acquaintances or strangers, that is, to people to whom we do not sense naturally any inclination to do good. It seems that for Hume, there is no need to promise anything to the members of our family or to our friends, given that we will do good to them spontaneously.[8]

Why do promises oblige for Hume? The obligation is solely due to the sanction attached to not maintaining one's word, which is simply this: one will no longer be able to profit from the institution of promising in the future. "When a man says *he promises any thing,* he in effect expresses a *resolution* of performing it; and along with that, by making use of this *form of words,* subjects himself to the penalty of never being trusted again in case of failure."[9] People who fail to keep their promises will no longer be able to convince others that it is in their interest to help them and thus they will be left without assistance when they need it. It is hence not immoral not to keep a promise; it is rather imprudent and unwise. One will only hurt oneself, at least in the long run.

Thomas Hobbes's approach to promising is similar. For him, too, the promise is a creation of society aiming at its benefit. Unlike Hume, however, he does not align the sanction for breaking a promise simply with the risk of not being trusted in the future. Given that the institution of promising is of paramount importance for the State, Leviathan imposes the obligation created by a promise with the concrete threat of punishment: "Covenants, without the sword, are but words, and of no strength to secure a man at all."[10] Why do I promise? Again, to make people do what I want them to do. Why do I keep my promises? Because otherwise I will have to pay a fine or be put to jail.

Why do we mention these two accounts here? It seems that this legalistic understanding of promising as social convention is still with us today

8. See ibid., 335: "Tho' this self-interested commerce of man begins to take place, and to predominate in society, it does not entirely abolish the more generous and noble intercourse of friendship and good offices. I may still do services to such persons as I love, and am more particularly acquainted with, without any prospect of advantage; and they may make me a return in the same manner, without any view but that of recompensing my past services. In order, therefore, to distinguish those two different sorts of commerce, the interested and the disinterested, there is a *certain form of words* invented for the former, by which we bind ourselves to the performance of any action" (original emphasis).

9. Ibid. (original emphases).

10. Hobbes, *Leviathan,* Part II, Chapter 17, 111.

much more than we may think. Here, a promise is something completely impersonal. The one to whom the promise is made never enters into the picture. A promise has nothing to do with love of the other. The fidelity, if such it is, involved in promising here is but a fidelity to the institution of promising, and ultimately only to the utility of this institution. From this perspective, it becomes difficult to see how a society's competent authority could not dispense someone of any and all promises made, given that the obligatory nature of these promises resides solely in the threat of sanction imposed precisely by this authority.

The "bond" created by the promise is an external obligation imposed by society for the sake of its general and impersonal benefit but, in given cases, this bond or this obligation—however good for society—may be to the detriment of the individual, who, by promising perhaps did not manage to obtain the benefit he or she had hoped for and that was the motive of the promise in the first place. Hence, it would only seem humane in these cases for the competent authority to release such a one from the bond or obligation created by the promise.

The Promise as Fidelity to Oneself in Kant and Nietzsche

The following two accounts of promising seem to be diametrically opposed to the previous ones. In Kant and Nietzsche one gets the idea that society is not needed at all for promises to exist. For Kant, while it is perhaps not all that clear why we promise in the first place, it is evident that the obligation to keep our promises derives from an application of the categorical imperative with its universalizability principle: "I ought never to act except in such a way *that I could also will that my maxim should become a universal law.*"[11] While prior to reflecting about it, I could feel tempted to get myself out of trouble by means of a promise I do not intend to keep, I could not well want lying to become the law of the land. Such a custom would be unreasonable, amounting to abolishing the institution of promising.[12] Thus we can say

11. Kant, *Groundwork*, 70 (original emphasis).

12. See ibid., 70–71: "Suppose I seek, however, to learn in the quickest way and yet unerringly how to solve the problem 'Does a lying promise accord with duty?' I have then to ask myself 'Should I really be content that my maxim (the maxim of getting out of a difficulty by a false promise) should hold as a universal law (one valid both for myself and others)? . . . I then become aware at once that I can indeed will to lie, but I can by no means will a universal law of lying; for by such a law there could properly be no promises at all."

that for Kant the obligation to keep my word derives from reason's necessity not to contradict itself, which means that the fidelity implied in promising is ultimately *a fidelity to myself as a rational agent.*

It is true that Kant's confidence in his universalizability principle seems to be exaggerated. It may at times serve as a heuristic principle and thus amount to no more than the common sense question: What would happen if everyone did this? But as ultimate foundation of morality it may well be wanting. Its greatest weakness is that it cannot answer the question of motivation: Why should I *want* to be rational, or be consistent with myself, which for Kant would be the same as to be moral and just? This problem was raised by the poet Walt Whitman who famously wrote: "I contradict myself? Very well then, I contradict myself; I am large, I contain multitudes."[13] But also Jürgen Habermas, a philosopher and contemporary follower of Kant's, shows that he is quite aware of this issue.[14]

Furthermore, as Alasdair MacIntyre points out, the universalizability principle already encounters grave difficulties on a much more obvious level. MacIntyre argues, and it seems rightly so, that "it is very easy to see that many immoral and trivial non-moral maxims are vindicated by Kant's test quite as convincingly—in some cases more convincingly—than the moral maxims which Kant aspires to uphold. So 'Keep all your promises throughout your entire life except one,' 'Persecute all those who hold false religious beliefs' and 'Always eat mussels on Mondays in March' will all pass Kant's test, for all can be consistently universalized."[15] The foundation of the moral obligation for promise-keeping would therefore seem a little thin in Kant.

What perhaps weighs still heavier is an element his account shares with that of Hume and Hobbes: the person to whom the promise is made is rather disregarded. Promising is not an inter-subjective reality and it has nothing

---

To inform myself in the shortest and yet infallible way about the answer to this problem, whether a lying promise is in conformity with duty, I ask myself: would I indeed be content that my maxim (to get myself out of difficulties by a false promise) should hold as a universal law (for myself as well as for others) . . . ? Then I soon become aware that I could indeed will the lie, but by no means a universal law to lie; for in accordance with such a law there would properly be no promises at all."

13. Whitman, "Song of Myself," 85.

14. See Habermas, *Future of Human Nature,* 4: "Moral insights effectively bind the will only when they are embedded in an ethical self-understanding that joins the concern about one's own well-being with the interest in justice. Deontological theories after Kant may be very good at explaining how to ground and apply moral norms; but they still are unable to answer the question of why we should be moral *at all*" (original emphasis).

15. MacIntyre, *After Virtue,* 45–46.

to do with the love of the other. While for Hume and Hobbes the obligation created by the promise resides in the relation between individual and State, in Kant this obligation is based on the relation of the rational agent with him- or herself. For Kant a promise is an intra-subjective reality.

This last point holds true also for Friedrich Nietzsche, which is why we have grouped him together with Kant here. In his *Genealogy of Morals*, Nietzsche dedicates a substantive section to the question of "breeding . . . an animal which is *entitled to make promises*,"[16] suggesting that the capacity to promise can function as the specific difference of the human being with respect to the animals[17] and presenting it as a privilege rather than a duty. To be able to give one's word as something that can be trusted is a major accomplishment of the will. It is here that we have the case of the sovereign individual, who has "his own independent, enduring will, the man who is *entitled to make promises*. And in him we find a proud consciousness, tense in every muscle, of what has finally been achieved here, of what has become incarnate in him—a special consciousness of power and freedom."[18] The "liberated man, who is really *entitled* to make promises, this master of *free* will," is the "the owner of an enduring, indestructible will."[19] What distinguishes him from others is that he "gives his word as something which can be relied on, because he knows himself strong enough to uphold it even against accidents, even 'against fate.'"[20] For Nietzsche the promise is "the memory of the will,"[21] and it is in the will that we find both the reason for making promises and the reason for keeping them. We are motivated to promise inasmuch as it is a splendid occasion to exercise our power—which for Nietzsche is why we do everything we do. The obligation to keep our promises derives from our desire for greatness and sovereignty. To break one's promise means to be servile, weak, and non-sovereign, dependent on the whims of circumstance and changing passion. In other words, it is a question of honor.

Indeed, the capacity to promise reveals much about the human being's personhood as someone who possesses him- or herself and is, as such, able

16. Nietzsche, *Genealogy of Morals*, 39 (original emphasis).

17. See Arendt, *Human Condition*, 245: "Nietzsche, in his extraordinary sensibility to moral phenomena, and despite his modern prejudice to see the source of all power in the will power of the isolated individual, saw in the faculty of promises (the 'memory of the will,' as he called it) the very distinction which marks off human from animal life."

18. Nietzsche, *Genealogy of Morals*, 41 (original emphasis).

19. Ibid. (original emphases).

20. Ibid.

21. Ibid., 40.

to anticipate the future.[22] Someone who were to say, "Yesterday I promised you to do this and that, but so what? Today I'm someone else," would simply disappear as a person. Thus, Robert Spaemann can place the foundation and guarantee of the promise in the person him- or herself: "By speaking and demanding to be understood, one has engaged in the same personal relation that is presumed in each separate act of promising. The question of how to secure the promise no longer arises. The final security is the refusal to pose the question, a refusal already made when human beings recognize each other, and claim recognition from each other, as persons. The person is a promise,"[23] so that someone who is not wont to keep his promises "degrades himself, degrades the promise that he, as a person, is."[24]

The question of promising is indeed intimately bound up with the issue of personal identity, as Paul Ricoeur quite insightfully points out: "We can understand two different things by identity. One is the permanence of an immutable substance which time does not affect. . . . But there is another model of identity, one presupposed by our previous model of the promise. . . . The problem of the promise is precisely that of maintaining a self in the face of what Proust called the vicissitudes of the heart."[25] Hence we may say that Nietzsche is getting at something profoundly true: at least part of the reason we promise is to maintain our identity in time and part of the reason of its obligatory nature is truly our honor, a fidelity to ourselves.

Yet here, too, we have to ask ourselves about the role, if any, of the person *to whom* the promise is made. What is his or her importance? As Ricoeur himself points out: "The obligation to maintain one's self in keeping one's promises is in danger of solidifying into the Stoic rigidity of simple

22. See Spaemann, *Persons*, 223–24: "The practice of promising throws a shaft of light on what it is to be a person. . . . When we make an actual promise in history . . . we rise above our normal immersion in the stream of time. We do not leave it to the course of events to decide what we shall do at a given point in the future, nor do we leave it to whatever attitude or state of mind, whishes or priorities we may happen to have at that time."

23. Ibid., 223. For a clarification of the suggestive idea that the person *is* a promise, see Spaemann and Zaborowski, "An Animal That Can Promise," 515: "We are natural beings like other living things that have wishes and desires and pleasure and fear and dread, and at the same time, we are beings that can relate themselves to this nature. Within this relation lies the promise that the person is, that a being, which can also feel a duty toward another, then also fulfills this duty—for that we have no guarantee; but rather, this is a promise."

24. Spaemann and Zaborowski, "Animal That Can Promise," 516.

25. Ricoeur, "Approaching the Human Person," 53.

constancy, if it is not permeated by the desire to respond to an expectation, even to a request coming from another."[26] Nietzsche's approach would entirely seem to fall under this criticism, since here it does not seem to matter to whom the promise is made.

Incidentally, as Gabriel Marcel incisively explains, for an account along the lines of Nietzsche, it does not even seem important *what* is being promised:

> To make it a point of honour to fulfil a commitment what else is this but putting an accent on the supra-temporal identity of the subject who contracts it and carries it out? And so I am brought to think that this identity has a validity in itself, whatever the content of my promise may be. This identity is the one important thing to maintain, however absurd the particular commitment may appear, to the eyes of a spectator, through my rashness or weakness in undertaking it.[27]

In this context, then, Marcel sees the great danger of confusing fidelity with pride: "A fidelity to another of which I was myself the ground, the spring, and the centre . . . would expose . . . the lie at the heart of that existence which it shapes."[28] This lie consists in "the contention that fidelity, despite appearances, is never more than a mode of pride and self-regard," and it "unquestionably robs of their distinctive character the loftiest experiences that men think they have known."[29]

If what is at stake in promising is simply a *fidelity to myself* in terms of a desire for self-consistency as in Kant, or in terms of a sense of honor as in Nietzsche, then it is I myself who can also dispense myself from my promise. Others could come to my aid by trying to help me see that keeping a word once given has now become unreasonable given the new circumstances. They could tell me to swallow my pride, admit my failure, and go on with my life.

The Promise as Inter-subjective Reality in Aquinas, Marcel, and Ricoeur

26. Ricoeur, *Oneself as Another*, 267.

27. Marcel, *Being and Having*, 53.

28. Ibid., 54.

29. Ibid., 53.

A Commitment to the Other

It is truly curious how the philosophers we have mentioned above, while taking into account important and valid aspects of promising, were nonetheless able to disregard its probably most important characteristic: a promise is inherently a promise *to* someone. Even Paul Ricoeur thinks that "it is easy to overlook" what he calls the "dyadic structure of promising," and he surmises that perhaps "Kant contributed to this by his treatment of the false promise as an inner contradiction to a maxim in which a person involves only himself or herself."[30] But is it truly so difficult to see that it is not *fear* of punishment (Hobbes) or of disadvantage (Hume) or of self-contradiction (Kant) or of the admittance of weakness (Nietzsche) but rather love of the other that is at the basis of the obligatory nature of promises? In this very sense Ricoeur continues: "It is, in truth, at the very first stage, that of firm intention, that the other is implied: a commitment that did not involve doing something that the other could choose or prefer would not be more than a silly wager."[31] Fidelity to one's word is fidelity to the one to whom one has given it. It is motivated not by fear but by love of him or her.

Not even Guy Mansini, in his *Promising and the Good*—a work that is otherwise extremely helpful—quite managed to get himself to speak about the love of the other as primary motive for keeping one's promises. Rather, Mansini's main thesis is that the binding nature of promises derives from the *good* that one promises.[32] The more this thesis is sustained by examples, the more improbable it becomes, at least if taken literally. Thus he writes: "The obligation to go to the post office on someone's behalf comes from the good of doing just that thing."[33] Is the purported fact that going to the post office is good really the reason for why one should keep one's promise to do so on someone else's behalf? How could going to the post-office be good in the first place if it were not good *for someone*?

It seems that it is the *other*, to whom we have made a pledge and who now relies on us, who is the primary reason for why we should keep our promises. It is a question of fidelity to him or her. Here Gabriel Marcel really seems to get at the heart of what is at stake in giving one's word:

30. Ricoeur, *Oneself as Another*, 266.

31. Ibid., 267.

32. Mansini, *Promising and the Good*, x: "The obligation to keep promises is not an artifact of the will of the one who promises. . . . The source of the obligation to fidelity to promises is chiefly the good promised."

33. Ibid., 38.

There is no commitment purely from my own side; it always implies that the other being has a hold over me. All commitment is a response. A one-sided commitment would not only be rash but could be blamed as pride. The notion of pride, indeed, plays a part of paramount importance in this discussion. It seems to me that it is essential to show that pride cannot be the principle upon which fidelity rests. As I see it, and despite appearances to the contrary, fidelity is never fidelity to one's self, but is referred to what I called the hold the other being has over us.[34]

Fidelity to one's word is fidelity to someone else, to a friend, to the beloved; it is a response to someone. In promising then, I am not primarily bound by society, the State, my logic or my honor, though all these surely enter in various degrees, but I am bound to the *other*, in whom I have raised expectations and who now relies on me.

Why We Promise

Why do we promise, then? For Thomas Aquinas there is more than one answer, but the first and foremost reason is that we promise to others for their good: "We promise something to a man for his own profit; since it profits him that we should be of service to him, and that we should at first assure him of the future fulfilment of that service."[35] Here we need to underline that the Angelic Doctor's anthropological presuppositions are very different from those of Hume's, for instance. For the British empiricist all human beings are naturally selfish. For St. Thomas, in contrast, "it is natural to all men to love each other."[36] With this he does not mean that people are not capable of hatred or selfishness; it just means that it is these latter that need explanation and not love and benevolence, which are natural and spontaneous. Now "love consists especially in this, that the lover wills the good for his loved one."[37] Not only the thing promised, but the promise itself is already a good, inasmuch as it virtually contains within it the thing promised, which is "why we thank not only a giver, but also one who promises to give."[38] Promises are among the goods we wish for the people we love.

34. Marcel, *Being and Having*, 46.

35. Aquinas, *Summa Theologica*, II-II, 88, 4.

36. Aquinas, *Summa Contra Gentiles*, III, 117, 6.

37. Ibid., III, 90, 6.

38. See Aquinas, *Summa Theologica*, II-II, 88, 5, ad 2: "He who promises something

In which way is a promise, already prior to its actual fulfillment, a good for the beloved? According to Hannah Arendt, promises establish "islands of certainty in an ocean of uncertainty."[39] Through promises people can coordinate their activity. It is true that promises are useful for the individual and for society. We could imagine a match between two soccer teams. In one team, players have agreed to play on certain positions: one promised to guard the goal, others committed to defensive tasks, still others agreed to play in midfield or forward positions. Meanwhile, the players on the other team were not able to agree on their positions; no one made a commitment to the other to cover a certain position, so they leave things up to the way each player feels at the moment. As a result, they end up entering the field without even an assigned goalie. If we suppose that all the players on both teams have similar individual capacities, then there will be no question as to which team will win. As Hannah Arendt keeps insisting, in order to achieve anything significant in life, people have to act together,[40] and they can act together, only if they are bound together by mutual promises. Thus, people benefit from promises collectively the moment they enter into a common endeavor.

But already an individual simply receiving a promise earns a decisive advantage as it will be possible "to rely on its performance, so as to be able to presume upon it safely in his or her own plans for action."[41] Anyone who has ever needed to organize an event will know the difference between a collaborator who responds to a request for a particular kind of aid with the words, "If I get a chance, perhaps I will do it," and the one who says, "I will be there, and I will do it." Only the latter words are a real help. Only here the person in charge can consider the task done, and stop looking for someone to whom to delegate it and attend to other duties.

---

gives it already in as far as he binds himself to give it: even as a thing is said to be made when its cause is made, because the effect is contained virtually in its cause. This is why we thank not only a giver, but also one who promises to give."

39. Arendt, *Human Condition*, 244.

40. See ibid., 244–45: "We mentioned before the power generated when people gather together and 'act in concert' . . . The force that keeps them together . . . is the force of mutual promise or contract. . . . The sovereignty of a body of people bound and kept together, not by an identical will which somehow magically inspires them all, but by an agreed purpose for which alone the promises are valid and binding, shows itself quite clearly in its unquestioned superiority over those who are completely free, unbound by any promises and unkept by any purpose."

41. Spaemann, *Persons*, 225.

The promise is the good that the lover wills for the beloved. We promise because we love. However, as much as we love the other, we may still consider whether a promise is an *adequate* good to give him or her. Is it morally licit to promise? Aquinas poses himself the objection that our freedom is the greatest good that God has given to us, and it would seem inappropriate deliberately to deprive ourselves of it by placing our will under necessity.[42] Gabriel Marcel even goes so far as to raise the question whether there is not a sense in which every promise is a lie:

> At the moment of my commitment, I either (1) arbitrarily assume a constancy in my feelings which it is not really in my power to establish, or (2) I accept in advance that I shall have to carry out, at a given moment, an action which will in no way reflect my state of mind when I do carry it out. In the first case I am lying to myself, in the second I consent in advance to lie to someone else.[43]

I have no power over how I will feel tomorrow. If I tell a friend today that I will come to visit him tomorrow because today that seems to me a good thing, I may betray my friend if tomorrow the visit no longer appears good to me and I no longer feel like it. If I go anyway, I will be insincere; if I do not go at all, I will have gone against my word, and the promise, to the extent that it implied not only an exterior behavior but a personal involvement, will be broken in any case, if not by my omission, then by my insincerity.

Furthermore, given that I am constantly changing, by promising perhaps I betray my future self, the person that I am becoming, of whom I do not know yet whether he should then want to be burdened by the commitments I make now.[44] Again, the question is raised, "Can a commitment exist that is not a betrayal?"[45]

---

42. See Aquinas, *Summa Theologica*, II-II, 88, 4, ad 1: "It would seem that it is not expedient to take vows. It is not expedient to anyone to deprive himself of the good that God has given him. Now one of the greatest goods that God has given man is liberty whereof he seems to be deprived by the necessity implicated in a vow."

43. Marcel, *Being and Having*, 50. See also Ricoeur, *Oneself as Another*, 267–68, where this passage is discussed.

44. See Marcel, *Being and Having*, 51: "Is there, then, such a thing as a basic fidelity, a primal bond, which I break every time I make a vow . . . ? This primal bond can only be what some people have taught me to call fidelity to myself. Myself, they will say, is what I betray when I so bind myself. Myself: not my being but my becoming; not what I am today but what I shall perhaps be tomorrow."

45. Ibid.

We have presented these two objections together because they can be responded to by a single fundamental consideration, which, at the same time, highlights another important reason for why we promise. To begin with, let us consider the response St. Thomas gives to his objection, a response that has not lost any of its pertinence throughout the centuries. Aquinas claims that, by promising we do not lose our freedom but we actualize it. Freedom is freedom for the good, and the firmer the will is fixed on the good, the freer it is. Aquinas points to the fact that God and the saints cannot sin. For them this does not amount to a reduction of freedom but to its perfection.[46] By promising we give firmness to our will,[47] which is also one of the reasons why, according to the Angelic Doctor, an act done because of a vow or promise is better than the same act done without a prior binding of the will. In the former case the good is willed more firmly: "A vow fixes the will on the good immovably and to do anything of a will that is fixed on the good belongs to the perfection of virtue."[48]

Here St. Thomas looks not only at the actual performance of an act but also at its genesis. An act born of a virtuous disposition is performed with more stability, joy, and ease than the same act done without such an active disposition, though from the outside it may be difficult to detect who is truly courageous and who is simply acting as a courageous person would do; who is truly temperate and who is merely continent. Likewise, an act that is generated by a promise is performed with greater stability and with a firmer will; hence it is more virtuous. Here we see that Nietzsche's account is not all wrong: being able to promise is an excellence, a virtue; it bespeaks a oneness with oneself, to the point that Paul Ricoeur makes of the promise a paradigm for personal identity as we have seen above.[49]

It is as if to the objection which Marcel puts himself, namely, that I must not promise because I do not know who I will be tomorrow, Aquinas along with Ricoeur would answer that I *must* promise so that I *will* know

46. See Aquinas, *Summa Theologica*, II-II, 88, 4, ad 1: "Even as one's liberty is not lessened by one being unable to sin, so, too, the necessity resulting from a will firmly fixed to good does not lessen the liberty, as instanced in God and the blessed."

47. See ibid., II-II, 88, 4: "By vowing we fix our wills immovably on that which it is expedient to do."

48. Ibid., II-II, 88, 6.

49. See Ricoeur, "Approaching the Human Person," 53. See also Ricoeur, *Oneself as Another*, 118: "When we speak of ourselves, we in fact have available to us two models of permanence in time which can be summed up in two expressions that are at once descriptive and emblematic: *character* and *keeping one's word*" (original emphases).

who I will be tomorrow. A promise is what allows me to maintain my personal identity over time; it is the way in which I relate to that part of my life that exists in the mode of anticipation of the future. A promise strengthens the will; it gives unity to the moral subject. As Robert Spaemann puts it, its goal is virtue, the capacity to rely on oneself.[50]

The Reasons for the Binding Power of Promises

Why, then, on this account, do promises bind? Paul Ricoeur can think of three reasons. There is indeed such a thing as my personal honor, which consists in maintaining a recognizable identity over time: "To keep a promise is to sustain oneself within the identity of one who today speaks and tomorrow will do. This sustaining oneself announces an esteem of self."[51] By breaking a promise I implicitly say that I am no longer the same now as I was then. I become invisible as a person, a being capable of owning and leading my life over time and become reduced to a Lockean self, who is but an accumulation of instances without inherent unity or continuity.

But there is, of course, also the *other* to whom the promise is made, who has a rightful expectation of me to do as I said, who relies on me: "One always makes a promise to someone . . . : it is because someone is counting on me and expecting me to keep my promise that I feel that I am connected."[52] To make a promise that I do not intend to keep or of which I do not know how I will be able to keep it, is to do him or her violence.[53] It is an act of injustice. A false or broken promise is not only a thing between me and an impersonal society, nor just a matter between me and myself, but first of all an issue between me and the other and of the love that governs inter-human relationships.

Third, for Ricoeur there is the respect I owe to the institution of language, which binds me to others and allows me to communicate: "The obligation to keep one's promise is equivalent to the obligation to preserve the institution of language to the extent that language rests on the confidence

50. See Spaemann, *Persons*, 225: "The purpose of this effort is what we call 'virtue': conditioning one's nature to reliable self-determination, integrating the various impulses with the goal of actually achieving what one wishes to achieve. What is at stake is the ability to rely on oneself."

51. Ricoeur, "Approaching the Human Person," 50.

52. Ibid.

53. See Ricoeur, *Oneself as Another*, 266: "The false promise is a figure of the evil of violence in the use of language, on the plane of interlocution (or of communication)."

everyone has in everyone else's word."[54] Language is oriented to truth; its purpose is to reveal reality, to be the "house of being."[55] It may not be a coincidence that in many languages the expression "to give one's word" is a synonym for "promising." By speaking, by saying a word to others, we promise them reality. Hence Erik Erikson can say, "A spoken word is a *pact*."[56] Indeed, the word binds us to being and binds us to each other. Such is our innate trust in the affirmative power of the word that says and affirms reality, that for the human mind it is much easier to understand affirmations than it is to understand negations and that our spontaneous attitude towards anything said or written is to believe it. Suspicion and mistrust are always secondary phenomena. Inasmuch as we are beings who "have the word,"[57] the institution of language mediates our access to reality; it allows us not only to relate to others but it is at the very foundation of our spiritual life, allowing for our thought to be actualized. Romano Guardini formulates it in these terms:

> Man by his nature is in a dialogue. His mental life is ordained to be in communication. . . . Language is not only the means by which we communicate conclusions, but mental life and activity are carried on in the process of speech. . . . Language is not a system of signs by means of which two monads exchange ideas but it is the very realm of consciousness in which every man lives.[58]

Thus we see why the institution of language deserves to be respected, why promises are not to be taken lightly and why they are binding. While Ricoeur's appeal to the institution of language echoes Hume's and Hobbes's appeal to society, inasmuch as language is a social reality, what the French thinker is trying to get at goes much beyond the concerns of the British philosophers. What is at stake is not simply a social convention but the very possibility of having conventions in the first place, i.e., the possibility itself of forming a society, of entering into relationship with oneself and with others.

On this account, then, which takes into consideration the dyadic structure of promising—i.e., the basic fact that promises are *to* someone—what

54. Ricoeur, "Approaching the Human Person," 50.

55. See Heidegger, *Pathmarks*, 254.

56. Erikson, "Problem of Ego Identity," 70 (original emphasis).

57. See Aristotle, *Politics*, I, 1, 1253a10: "Man alone of all the animals possesses speech." On this also see Taylor, *The Language Animal*.

58. Guardini, *World and the Person*, 130.

is the nature of the bond? The bond would seem to reside in or even *be* the relationship between the one who gives and the one who receives the promise. The obligation is *to the other*; we are *obliged* to the other because we love him or her, love being the reason we made our promise in the first place. It is the same love for the other that was the reason for making our promise that is now the reason for our keeping it.

This is certainly evident in our dealings with our family and friends. But how is this applicable to social interactions, such as contracts, which are forms of promises given also to strangers? Even here this account is valid if by love we do not understand a romantic feeling but the fundamental benevolence that governs the interaction between persons and their fellow human beings. Again, "it is natural to all men to love each other,"[59] that is, to wish each other well. Saint Thomas could say such a thing because he believed that the human person's greatest good was not an individual private good, but a common good.[60] My greatest good is precisely not just my good, but *our* good. If you are well, we are well, and therefore I am truly well only if we are well. Why should I still honor my part of the terms of a contract when the other has already fulfilled his or hers, and I got what I wanted? It is for the sake of the other's good that I do it, a good that can motivate me as much as my own. This is what Robert Spaemann implies when he writes, "At one time the concept of love was thought of as a metamorphosis of self-interests, as the self-transcendence of a rational being, on account of which the reality of the other in its own teleology immediately became a motive of action."[61] He then continues by referring to Leibniz' profound definition of benevolence: "*Delectatio in felicitate alterius*, 'Joy in the happiness of others.'"[62]

---

59. Aquinas, *Summa Contra Gentiles*, III, 117, 6.

60. St. Thomas argues that inasmuch as God is the common good of the universe, it is natural for a creature to love God more than it loves itself. See *Summa Theologica*, I, 60, 5: "Since God is the universal good, and under this good both man and angel and all creatures are comprised, because every creature in regard to its entire being naturally belongs to God, it follows that from natural love angel and man alike love God before themselves and with a greater love."

61. Spaemann, *Happiness and Benevolence*, 78.

62. Ibid. See Leibniz, *Codex Iuris Gentium*, 171.

Dispensations

Under which conditions, then, can one be dispensed from one's promises? If keeping one's promise is primarily an act of fidelity not to the State or to oneself, but to the other, then it is the other who can normally dispense. Dispensation may be asked for on account of new, supervening circumstances that make fulfilling one's promise significantly more difficult or cause it to collide with unforeseen new obligations. At times, we even dispense ourselves, when the other is not at hand or when he or she unreasonably insists on the fulfillment of a promise given under completely different circumstances. As Spaemann puts it, "Of course, there are promises from which we excuse ourselves on the ground of urgent necessity that imposes duties inconsistent with them."[63] If I am heading for a dinner appointment and on the way become witness of an accident, suddenly finding myself called upon to aid the people involved in it, I can reasonably count on the others to dispense me from my promise to be at a certain place at a certain time. Without entering into a casuistry, however, we can insist with Spaemann that one thing can *never* be the ground for a dispensation: "It can never be a reason for non-performance that the promiser simply asserts that he has changed his mind."[64] Given that, as Ricoeur puts it, a promise is a redoubled intention: "the intention not to change my intention,"[65] the not-changing one's mind was exactly the content of the promise.

The Marital Promise and Other "Life Promises"

In the following section, we will ask ourselves what is special about the marital promise. Doing so, we will also touch upon what Guy Mansini aptly calls "life promises" in general.[66]

The Specificity of the Marital Promises: Forming a Community of Destiny

For Spaemann, what distinguishes a marital promise from other promises is that its irrevocability is part of the content of what is being promised,

63. Spaemann, *Persons*, 226.
64. Ibid.
65. Ricoeur, *Oneself as Another*, 268.
66. See Mansini, *Promising and the Good*, 71–83 and 137–44.

with the result that here two people form a "community of destiny."[67] What makes us request dispensations of our promises, and what makes us gladly grant these if we are being asked for them, are the strides of fate: new, unforeseeable circumstances that change the whole context in which a promise was made. Now the marital promise is a promise by which the spouses tell each other: *whatever* may happen, whatever destiny holds in store for us, I pledge my fidelity to you, in sickness or health, for better or worse. Thus by the very intention of the promise, the spouses give each other an *unconditional* pledge. By saying, "in good times and in bad . . . until death do us part" the spouses promise each other not to ask to be dispensed nor to dispense each other.

The nature of the marital promise is such that it radically changes the spouses' relationship. Its idea is that it is capable of turning strangers into kin. Even if husband and wife were mutually to agree on dispensing each other from their marital vows, this could not be done, inasmuch as their vows have instituted between them a relation of kinship that is no longer in their power to change.[68] The case is similar to that of a father and a son who wanted to dispense each other from their father-son relationship. They would be attempting the impossible. The kinship established by the biological fact of generation ensures that the father remains the father; the son remains the son. And this is true even if the kinship is established by the legal act of adoption. The idea of marriage is that a marital promise can establish kinship as well, so that Adam, after having been led to Eve, can say in all truth: "This at last is bone of my bones and flesh of my flesh" (Gen 2:23)—which means saying precisely: "She is my kin."

How is it possible to make such a promise? Can one truly build a common life in the face of fate? Very often in life things happen that are completely out of our power: illness, infertility, economic difficulties, problems with the children. In this situation—called the general human condition—how is it possible to promise one's life, including also what one will want in the future, and not just the authenticity of one's emotions, including only what one feels in the present?

Here Robert Spaemann offers us a profound reflection when he suggests that by exchanging marital vows, the spouses do not simply commit

67. See Spaemann, *Persons*, 228, where the English translation speaks of a "lifelong sharing of destinies." The original German, however, speaks of a "lifelong community of destiny," a "lebenslange Schicksalsgemeinschaft"; see Spaemann, *Personen*, 243.

68. See Hahn, *Kinship by Covenant*.

to hang on to their promise with an iron will, even if they should come to feel differently, even if they should come to regret their choice and change their minds.[69] Rather, the marital promise implies the promise to do everything in one's power to prevent coming into situations that would incline one to reconsider one's commitment to the other. While our feelings are not under our immediate control, our day-to-day decisions are. It is by the big and small choices we make every day that we develop our character and personality. We are constantly changing and our choices are a major factor in this process. According to Spaemann, then, the marital promises imply not viewing "the growth of one's personality as an independent variable that may or may not turn out to be compatible in some degree with the growth of the other's personality."[70] Thus the question, "What effect will such and such a choice have on the relationship with my spouse?" will become the decisive criterion for any decision that a married person will have to make. By assuming the married state, a person freely renounces the privilege of making choices solely on the basis of personal preference. If, as a single person, I live in Rome and get a job offer in the United States, the only question I need to ask is whether I would like the job or not. If I am married I will also need to ask my wife if she wants to move with me, and if not, what it would mean for our relationship to leave her in another country and come home to her just once a month. These are the kind of choices that are entirely entrusted to our freedom and that make our marriages work out or fail.

In the journey of a common life, however, there will always be some things that truly just happen, events that are completely unrelated to our prior choices and for which we carry no responsibility at all. But even here, a married couple is not entirely at the mercy of fate. While by definition we cannot choose what merely happens, we can always choose how to respond to it. As Spaemann writes, "Marriage is predicated on the capacity of persons to create a structure for their life that is independent of unforeseen occurrences, delivering themselves from the control of chance by deciding

69. Spaemann, *Persons*, 226–27: "Marriage is no ordinary promise to perform something, which one can still go through with when one has no mind to, or no longer feels the special interest that inclined one to the promise in the first place. With the marriage vow two people tie their fortunes together irrevocably—or that, at any rate, is what the vow intends. This promise could hardly be kept if one were in fact to change one's mind fundamentally."

70. Ibid., 227.

once and for all in advance how such occurrences will be dealt with."[71] Being married means that some options one would otherwise have to react to a blow of fate are closed. However, no longer having all the theoretical options open does not mean that one is no longer free. It just means that one's range of options has become delimited.[72] One could not possibly have actualized all the options anyway. Here the married person is not in a situation that is qualitatively different from the general human predicament: the moment we walk through one door, we close all the others. As Maurice Blondel convincingly points out, "we do not go forward, we do not learn, we do not enrich ourselves except by closing off for ourselves all roads but one and by impoverishing ourselves of all that we might have known or gained otherwise. . . . I must commit myself under the pain of losing everything."[73] Freedom is given to be given, and only by being given is it actualized. By wanting to keep all options open, we do not choose anything. But then soon enough all the options we had or thought we had will close themselves off just by themselves.

Life Promises in the Face of Death

The same holds true for the other kind of promises that are for life: religious vows or the promise of priestly celibacy. Here, too, people give definitive shape to their lives, by closing off all other roads but one; here, too, they have to deliberately cultivate their vocation, asking themselves how their individual small choices and bigger projects will impact their attitude toward their state of life. By making a life promise, whether it be making a marital promise, taking religious vows or promising priestly celibacy, we intend to dispose of our entire future, look at our life as a whole and thus, as Mansini rightly points out, already anticipate death.[74]

71. Ibid., 228.

72. See ibid., 227: "At every stage of one's growth one is aware of the meaning it has for the other and for the other's growth. This is a very considerable restriction of our room to manoeuvre, but it is not a restriction of our *freedom*. For we could not in any case exhaust the whole range of possibilities. With every possibility we choose, we cancel others. If we do not wish to pay that price, we can never grasp the possibilities we have, and so never actually realize freedom" (original emphasis).

73. Blondel, *Action*, 4.

74. Mansini, *Promising and the Good*, 76: "To promise something for life makes us contemplate death. When we marry, we contemplate the death of ourselves and our spouses. Priestly or religious promising also has us look forward to death."

For a culture in which people increasingly do not believe in eternal life and tend to think of death as total annihilation, the thought of death can only be frightening and paralyzing and will thus be avoided at all costs. Said the other way around: If I am unable to face the thought of death, then I will also be unable to look at my life as a whole and hence be unable to make a life promise.[75] I will be unable to promise "until death do us part," and be much prone to see my life as a succession of unrelated events without any inherent unity.

According to some authors, our present culture has fallen prey to a "chronological atomism," that is, "an understanding of life as composed of interchangeable and essentially identical units of time."[76] Forgetting that there is a life cycle may lead to bizarre situations. Thus, at one point Max Scheler recounts his strange encounter with an elderly man who behaved as if he were eighteen years old.[77] His was a case of a clinically attested mental illness, and yet many of our contemporaries live in an analogous way without actually having a mental problem. Their difficulty rather lies in their tendency to see life like a random sum of disparate parts, while instead life is more like a symphony, where each part, precisely in its difference from all the others, is related in a meaningful and quasi-necessary way to the whole, making the whole beautiful.[78]

Life Promises in a Vision of Fruitfulness

We would like to suggest that it is not only our contemporaries' intolerance of the thought of death that accounts for their inability to promise their

75. See ibid.: "If we are a people who cannot face death, as is commonly alleged, then we must also be a people who cannot face promising for life. Now, the passing of Christianity makes it harder for us to keep death daily before our eyes, since we think of it as personal annihilation. . . . If it really is true that I cannot look squarely at death, however, then I cannot really make a life promise."

76. President's Council on Bioethics, *Beyond Therapy*, 185.

77. See Scheler, "Repentance and Rebirth," 45: "In a German lunatic asylum, some years ago, I came across an old man of seventy who was experiencing his entire environment on the plane of development reached in his nineteenth year. That doesn't mean that the man was still lost amid the actual objects making up his world when he was a boy of eighteen, that he saw his home of those days, with its attendant people, streets, towns, etc. No, he saw, heard and experienced nothing but what was going on around him in the room, but he lived it all as the boy of eighteen he once was, with all that boy's individual and general impulses and ambitions, hopes and fears."

78. See President's Council on Bioethics, *Beyond Therapy*, 185.

lives. As Guy Mansini aptly puts it: "What is the same in marriage vows, priestly celibacy, and religious chastity . . . is that they all bear on the body and the sexuality of the body. Life promises, which look toward death, are dispositions of the procreative power that looks beyond it."[79] On the natural level, the response to our mortality is our fruitfulness[80] and it is no accident that life promises, in which we regard our lives as a whole, would dispose precisely of our capacity to be fruitful. While death is the end of life in the one sense of "end" (i.e., when it's over), fruitfulness is the end of life in the other sense (i.e., what gives meaning to it). It is not only if we shun the thought of death, but also if we no longer perceive an aim or end to give meaning to our lives that we will not be able to see our lives as a whole and to commit our entire lives in a promise. In other words, to be able to promise our lives, we need the sense of having a goal, a mission, a call to some kind of fruitfulness. As Pope Francis beautifully puts it, "Promising love for ever is possible when we perceive a plan bigger than our own ideas and undertakings, a plan which sustains us and enables us to surrender our future entirely to the one we love."[81]

The problem with contemporary culture that makes it so difficult for people to promise is that essentially they have lost the idea of love's fruitfulness. Jesus tells his disciples what we are entitled to believe he tells every human being: I "appointed you that you should go and bear fruit and that your fruit should abide" (John 15:16). Any composite reality derives its unity from its end or aim. Life can have a unity only if it has a purpose, an end, or goal. Jesus tells us that this purpose is fruitfulness, and prior to the modern age his words would have been self-evident to any reader or listener. There is more to life than just living. If there is nothing we desire more than living, then soon enough we will begin to loathe living. There is hardly anything that people desire more in their lives than a mission, something to live and possibly to die for.

Until recently it was very clear to people that this noble striving was naturally related to the family. Recognizing oneself as a son or daughter, one appreciates and accepts the original gift of life. Responding in gratitude to the gift of life that one has freely received, one becomes aware of a calling to pass this life on in love: to become husband and wife who together are

79. Mansini, *Promising and the Good*, 139.

80. See Kass, *Life, Liberty and the Defense of Dignity*, 273: "Children and their education . . . are life's—and wisdom's—answer to mortality."

81. Francis, *Lumen Fidei*, no. 52.

called to become father and mother.[82] For most people it is in the family that they begin to live for others, that they begin to respond to their innate vocation to a common life lived in a love that is fruitful. Love's fruitfulness then confirms the marital bond and is itself a reason for its indissolubility, inasmuch as the bond is oriented to being objectified in the common children, who, for their deepest identity, depend on the permanence of the relationship from which they sprang.

Also for those who receive the call to continence for the sake of the kingdom, this fundamental structure remains intact. They, too, are called to fruitfulness. It is not only the pleasures of intercourse that they renounce for the kingdom. They also renounce their earthly fruitfulness: to have a family and to have children of their own. Jesus's promise to them is a superabundant recompense precisely for *this* renunciation; theirs will be an abounding spiritual fruitfulness: "Truly, I say to you, there is no man who has left house or wife or brothers or parents or children, for the sake of the kingdom of God, who will not receive manifold more in this time, and in the age to come eternal life" (Luke 18:29). It is thus the question of fruitfulness and with this the question of life's meaningfulness that is at stake when it comes to life promises.

Conclusion

Let us briefly return to the question with which we have started. What meaning could it have to think of the marital bond "as a kind of metaphysical hypostasis beside or over the personal love of the spouses"?[83] It will have very little sense if we understand the promise that brings about this bond as a mere social convention (Hume) or as the expression of a will to be faithful to oneself (Nietzsche). Inasmuch, however, as a promise is essentially a pledge of fidelity *to the other* (Ricoeur, Marcel), it has the capacity of radically transforming a relationship.

The marital promise is by its very terms an unconditional pledge of fidelity. As such it turns a conditional relationship of friendship into an

---

82. See Benedict XVI, "Address to Participants in the Meeting Promoted by the Pontifical John Paul II Institute for Studies on Marriage and Family": "It is in the family that the human person discovers that he or she is not in a relationship as an autonomous person, but as a child, spouse or parent, whose identity is founded in being called to love, to receive from others and to give him or herself to others." See also Melina, *Building a Culture*, 17–19.

83. Kasper, *Gospel of the Family*, 16.

unconditional relationship of kinship: two friends become family. Without being something abstract floating in a Platonic heaven of ideas, the bond is still more than the personal love of the spouses understood in terms of their subjective feelings and affections. It is a particular kind of relationship that needs to be understood in a way that is analogous to other family relationships like fatherhood or motherhood. Whatever a man may feel for his son, whether he loves him or disowns him, he is still the father. Fatherhood is unconditional and independent of the personal love a father feels for his son. The same holds for all other family relationships. The bond between two people is their relationship, and the relationship is more than the personal affection that two people feel for each other; it is indeed an objective reality. There is a bond that is created by descent, and there is a bond created by promises.

And of course, this is all about personal love, but one, to be sure, that is greater than mere sentiment. It is this personal love that is the reason for the exchange of the promises; this love desires to commit itself, to pledge itself for all days to come. In this sense, then, it is true: the marital bond cannot be thought of apart from the spouses' personal love, inasmuch as the bond is the objectification of this love. It is a form, a stability, an "institution" that love gives to itself. This stable, unconditional relationship is the fruit of a love that has committed itself, and we can say that it *is* a relationship of love, quite independent of the spouses' subsequent personal, subjective feelings of affection.

Finally, there is indeed and most certainly a way in which the marital bond is metaphysically hypostatized in a quite literal way, insofar as this bond is ordered to fruitfulness in the flesh. We can say that the common children are the objectification of the bond, its "hypostasis" or metaphysical substance, just as we can call the children the incarnation of their parents' love. Marital promises create a particular bond that institutes an objective relationship that is independent of the spouses' subjective feelings and that is—precisely in its permanence—a relationship of fruitful love.

6

The Universal and the Concrete
—an Order for Love?

A Story

I N A CONVERSATION WITH a lady who asked him about the possibility
of active love, Zosima, the Elder in Dostoevsky's *Brothers Karamazov*,
recounts the story of an old physician who struggled with the following
problem:

> "I love humanity," he said, "but I wonder at myself. The more I
> love humanity in general, the less I love man in particular. In
> my dreams," he said, "I have often come to making enthusiastic
> schemes for the service of humanity . . . and yet I am incapable of
> living in the same room with any one for two days together, as I
> know by experience. . . . I become hostile to people the moment
> they come close to me. But it has always happened that the more
> I detest men individually the more ardent becomes my love for
> humanity."[1]

This experience of the old doctor touches at the heart of our question
about the universality and concreteness of love and the need for an order in
our loves. Today, in our globalized age, "humanity" seems to become ever
less an abstraction and ever more a concrete reality. We are united by the
modern means of travel and enjoy the benefits of instant communication
with people from all parts of the planet. When in China people develop a

1. Dostoevsky, *Brothers Karamazov*, 57.

taste for dairy products, people in Germany can immediately know about it and—due to an interconnected world-economy—must suffer higher milk prices for it.[2] With the institution of the United Nations a first step has been made to found an organization that represents humanity as a whole. With the International Court in Den Haag, humanity already has its international court, where "crimes against humanity" can be prosecuted. Some thinkers are considering the idea of a world parliament,[3] while others actively attempt to establish a "world ethic."[4] Having begun to be its own proper subject on the stage of world history, humankind may perhaps also qualify as an authentic object of our love and affection.

In this chapter I will argue that the hypostatization of humanity remains a temptation and a danger, maybe today more so than ever. It is a *temptation* because it is much safer and more comfortable to love abstract humanity instead of loving individual humans, and it is a temptation also because it feeds on our natural pride which is so concerned with making a difference in the overall scheme of things; it is a serious *danger* because in our concern for universal humanity we may easily lose sight of and forget concrete human beings with their absolute dignity. Moreover, I will make the case that in order to avoid the dangers of this abstraction, we will have to order our loves well.

A Temptation

It is our common experience that when we love someone, we are vulnerable. "Love anything," C. S. Lewis writes, "and your heart will certainly be wrung and possibly be broken."[5] More than anything, it is individual people who disappoint or betray us, who are ungrateful or forgetful, however the case may be. This is the problem which the lady with whom the Elder Zosima has engaged in dialogue is acutely aware of:

> "You see, I so love humanity that—would you believe it?—I often dream of forsaking all that I have. . . . But could I endure such a life for long?" the lady went on fervently, almost frantically. . . . "If the patient whose wounds you are washing did not meet you with gratitude, but worried you with his whims, without valuing

2. See for instance Bonstein et al., "Wer melkt wen?" 18–21.

3. See for instance Habermas, "Kant's Idea of Perpetual Peace," 165–202.

4. See Küng, *Global Responsibility.*

5. Lewis, *Four Loves,* 121.

or remarking your charitable services, began abusing you and rudely commanding you . . . what then? Would you persevere in your love, or not? And do you know, I came with horror to the conclusion that, if anything could dissipate my love to humanity, it would be ingratitude. In short, I am a hired servant, I expect my payment at once—that is, praise, and the repayment of love with love. Otherwise I am incapable of loving any one."[6]

We love and need to be loved in return. No other experience is as fulfilling and at the same time as dangerous and most likely painful as the experience of love.

Yet the fact is that humanity as such, while unlikely to show particular signs of gratitude, will at least not be ungrateful to us. It is not likely to disappoint us. The philanthropist who has grown sick and tired of people can still say, "I do it for the sake of humanity," though he may regret that humanity has so many human beings in it. Humanity in any case is a rather benign and safe object of our love, safer by all means than grudging, grumpy, and often quite intolerable humans.

Apart from our preference for playing it safe, there is a second reason for the temptation to make universal humanity the object of our love. It lies in our distaste for our own limitation and finiteness. We have a thirst for meaning. We need our lives and our actions to be meaningful. But the things that are meaningful seem to lie only on the big-scale, universal level. What is the point of giving alms to this individual poor person? Would it not be much more important to eradicate poverty? What is the point of this gesture of reconciliation with my neighbor when there is war all over the world? Individual acts of love or kindness seem to be pointless in the face of all the injustice in the world. We find that to make a difference, we need to work on the level not of people but of structures, eliminating or at least alleviating poverty, disease, and war as such; only in this way, it appears, we can ensure our lives to be meaningful.

A Danger

The principal danger with our love of humanity is for us to forget the individual over the universal, i.e., for the love of humanity to forget the love of humans, or even, in the extreme case, to sacrifice the individual to the universal. The conviction that, in fact, we are working for the good of humanity

6. Dostoevsky, *Brothers Karamazov*, 56.

as such may endow us with such an elevated sense of moral rectitude that we feel completely entitled to sacrifice this individual human being to the good of humankind as such, as is done for instance in the case of certain kinds of scientific experimentations performed on human embryos, which is certainly very bad for the embryos but presumably good for human progress. A similar forgetfulness of the individual led to the Marxist theory of impoverishment, which Benedict XVI refers to in *Deus Caritas Est*. According to this theory, concrete help given to individual people in need is a means of prolonging unjust social structures. Hence, in order to help humanity, one should precisely *not* offer any assistance so that, under the pressure of poverty, there will finally be a revolution which will cause these unjust structures to collapse. Severely criticizing this view, the pope writes:

> Seen in this way, charity is rejected and attacked as a means of preserving the *status quo*. What we have here, though, is really an inhuman philosophy. People of the present are sacrificed to the *moloch* of the future—a future whose effective realization is at best doubtful. One does not make the world more human by refusing to act humanely here and now.[7]

It is a sad fact that some of the most outrageous crimes against humanity were committed precisely by those who, on their own confession, were most concerned with humanity's progress. The abstraction from the individual and his or her absolute dignity leads to the temptation to sacrifice individual human beings for the sake of a better future of humanity. In this way, however, our efforts at establishing a better world easily turn into the attempt to eradicate poverty by eradicating the poor, as it was sometimes practiced by totalitarian regimes, or to eliminate suffering by eliminating those who are suffering, as is the case with the practice of euthanasia, for instance.

This side of heaven a human society of perfect justice without poverty and suffering will remain an illusion. Jesus himself tells us: "For you always have the poor with you, and whenever you will, you can do good to them" (Mark 14:7). And hence also Benedict XVI points out the limits of what can be done on the structural level of society, emphasizing that individual acts of love, charity, "will always prove necessary, even in the most just society." He continues:

---

7. Benedict XVI, *Deus Caritas Est*, no. 31.

There is no ordering of the State so just that it can eliminate the need for a service of love. Whoever wants to eliminate love is preparing to eliminate man as such. . . . There will always be situations of material need where help in the form of concrete love of neighbour is indispensable. The State which would provide everything, absorbing everything into itself, would ultimately become a mere bureaucracy incapable of guaranteeing the very thing which the suffering person—every person—needs: namely, loving personal concern. We do not need a State which regulates and controls everything, but a State which, in accordance with the principle of subsidiarity, generously acknowledges and supports initiatives arising from the different social forces and combines spontaneity with closeness to those in need.[8]

The way to the universal is the concrete. Mother Theresa, for instance, did not work out a strategy towards fighting unjust social structures but she helped individual people in need and in this way also helped change the structures, working for a world that is more humane, working, in fact, for the progress of humanity. The individual human being is not a mere instance of humanity and as such exchangeable and replaceable. Rather, as Robert Spaemann puts it, the individual person is the "real symbol" of the absolute,[9] the "one represents the whole."[10] When I encounter him or her, I encounter humanity, and the only place where I encounter humanity is in him or her. Hence, the individual lays an absolute claim on me. It is the claim of humanity as such, fully present in this particular person. We are reminded of the wisdom of our Jewish brothers who say that "Whoever saves a single life—it is as though he has saved the entire world."[11]

A Motivation

If our call is to love the concrete, the individual, then first we have to ask how we can overcome the two temptations that we talked about in the

8. Ibid., no. 28.

9. See Spaemann, *Happiness and Benevolence*, 107: "The relationship between love of God and 'love of neighbor,' on the other hand, does not have a transcendental form and is not a case of categorical application; rather it concerns the presence of the absolute and its real symbol."

10. See ibid., 109.

11. Inscription on the "Medal of the Righteous," taken from the *Mishnah*, Sanhedrin 4:5.

beginning: love of this concrete human being tends to be rather tiresome, and compared to humanity as a whole, this particular human person seems insignificant. I would like to suggest that to both of these temptations we can respond with the following exhortation adapted from Hannah Arendt: *Remember birth.* What does remembering our birth do? First of all, it reminds us of the gift received. In her book on the concept of love in St. Augustine, Arendt writes:

> The decisive fact determining man as a conscious, remembering being is birth or "natality," that is, the fact that we have entered the world through birth. . . . Gratitude for life having been given at all is the spring of remembrance . . . What ultimately stills the fear of death is not hope or desire, but remembrance and gratitude.[12]

Having entered the world through birth, we have received a gift: the gift of our very existence. We have received a gift, we have been loved first. We love because we have been loved. As Benedict XVI puts it: "Since God has first loved us (cf. 1 Jn 4:10), love is now no longer a mere 'command'; it is the response to the gift of love with which God draws near to us."[13] Hence, the motivation at the root of our love profoundly changes. It becomes gratitude, which for Spaemann is the essential character of finite beings' benevolence.[14] Remembering my birth thus means acknowledging the gift of my existence and letting my every activity, my every act of love and kindness be informed by gratitude. In the spirit of this gratitude, I can be generous and merciful even to the "ungrateful and selfish," just as my heavenly Father is (see Luke 6:35–36).

Apart from filling me with a sense of gratitude, remembering my birth reminds me of my contingency and my constitutive limitedness. I did not make myself but I depend on others for my existence. In birth I came into being under entirely contingent and particular circumstances. I am born to specific people at a particular place on earth at a specific time in history. At the same time my existence remains forever marked and characterized by the peculiar conditions of its coming into being. Human existence is

12. Arendt, *Love and Saint Augustine*, 51–52. For a discussion of this text and for an examination of the role of Augustine's thought in Hannah Arendt, see Kampowski, *Arendt, Augustine and the New Beginning.*

13. Benedict XVI, *Deus Caritas Est*, no. 1.

14. Spaemann, *Happiness and Benevolence*, 108. See also Larrú, "Original Source of Love," 202: "Finding ourselves in a constitutive relationship with our Creator makes us grateful for all we have received, beginning with the gift of life. This gratitude becomes the very first form of human love."

conditioned existence, and birth, along with death, is among its most basic conditions.[15] Remembering our birth in a sense forces us to be reconciled to our finiteness and conditionedness. Once we are able to accept our being as finite and conditioned, we will also be able to accept our activity as finite and conditioned without thereby calling it meaningless. We will remember the worth of what is concrete and individual, since we ourselves are concrete individuals.

An Order

The moment we do turn our love to individual concrete human beings, however, an order is necessary. The need for an order derives first of all from the simple fact that what we love is always more than one thing. If we simply loved humanity, which is just one, an order might not be necessary, but if we love concrete human beings, which are necessarily several, the matter is different: any kind of relation to several things needs an order. Besides, if to love means to will the good for someone,[16] we soon find that the goods with which we love other people are limited. And even in a utopian Marxist society of superabundance where produced goods are held in such superabundance that there is no more need for distributive justice,[17] an order of love would still be necessary because the strictly personal goods such as our time, effort, and attention will always be as limited as we ourselves are. Finally, the goods that we wish to other persons in loving them are different in kind. There are goods that one appropriately wishes to one's wife, while the goods one suitably wishes to one's colleagues will be different in kind. The different qualities of the goods involved in our love also necessitate an order

---

15. See Arendt, *Human Condition*, 7–9.

16. See Aquinas, *Summa Contra Gentiles*, III, 90, 6: "Love consists especially in this, 'that the lover wills the good for his loved one.'" Thomas cites from Aristotle, *Rhetoric*, II, 4.

17. See Spaemann, *Basic Moral Concepts*, 36–37: "The peculiar thing about Karl Marx's vision of the future is that it is not concerned with justice, but with setting up a situation where there is no more need for justice, a situation where there is abundance and everyone can just help themselves without there being any need to pay. The production of goods in this state of abundance should take up so little time that there would be no need for the criteria of justice even in the distribution of work time. This situation would be called 'communism' and in it the principle 'to each according to his needs' would hold sway."

in our loves.[18] This *ordo amoris* is so crucial that ultimately, as Max Scheler points out, it defines who we are.[19] For Augustine, the order of love is the very definition of virtue; virtue, for him, is well-ordered love.[20]

Where does the order come from and what does it look like? Let us examine for a moment the parable of the Good Samaritan. In fact, the question of the right *ordo amoris* seems to be more or less co-extensive with the question of who is my neighbor. Here, the parable at first sight appears precisely to abolish the order in favor of a universal brotherhood of humankind. We have a stranger lending help to a stranger. And yet, at a closer look we see that the parable does not teach that in fact everyone *is* my neighbor, burdening me with a universal responsibility for humanity as such—the danger of which we have discussed above. Rather, it says that everyone *can become* my neighbor, namely anyone who is in fact close to me and who happens to be in need of my help here and now, independent of his or her social status, race, or religion.[21] In this way, "The concept of 'neighbour' is now universalized, yet it remains concrete" as Benedict XVI says, commenting on the parable.[22] The first principle of the *ordo amoris* thus seems to be the nearness or farness of the other person. All things being equal, we are more responsible for the people closer to us, while this closeness can imply literal physical closeness—as in the case of the parable—or personal closeness, such as is involved in family relations. If I were to find myself in the tragic situation of having to choose whether to save my own son or the son of a stranger, I will certainly save my son.[23]

Implicit in the parable is yet another principle of order, namely that of *urgency*[24]: It is likely that the Priest and the Levite did not randomly

18. See Noriega, "Love and Reason," 126–41.

19. Scheler, "Ordo amoris," 100: "*Whoever has the* ordo amoris *of a man has the man himself.* . . . He sees through him as far as one possibly can" (original emphasis).

20. See Augustine, *City of God,* XV, 22: "A brief and true definition of virtue is 'rightly ordered love.'"

21. See Spaemann, *Happiness and Benevolence,* 112: "The Samaritan is a foreigner who comes by chance across a man who needs his help. He is the one who happens to be close by. This situation does not somehow exempt one from the *ordo amoris*; rather it is a case for its application."

22. Benedict XVI, *Deus Caritas Est,* no. 15.

23. See Spaemann, *Happiness and Benevolence,* 111.

24. See Pérez-Soba, "Love of God and Love of Neighbor," 313: "There are people to whom we are especially close, and we have a moral duty to grow in our love for them. On the other hand, we need to know how to respond effectively to certain extraneous needs. The two criteria are different and can lead to different preferences in different

refuse to help out of mere laziness or indifference, but that they had a very precise motivation *not to act*. Helping the man fallen among the robbers would have put them in danger of becoming ritually unclean, namely in the case that the man had already been dead or had died on them, which as ministers of religious rites they wanted to avoid as much as possible. The criticism that the parable thus raises against them is that they failed to see that in their particular situation helping their neighbor in danger of death was more urgent than avoiding ritual impurity.

Finally, the particular goods at stake function as principles of order. To love means to will the good for the other. The particular kinds of goods that we wish for each other determine the nature of the relationship and possess their own objective truth.[25] The goods of a conjugal friendship— for instance, wishing for your wife the good of motherhood—are different from the goods involved in a professional friendship—for example, wishing your friend to be successful in her work. The moment a mother starts loving her son as if he were her husband or the moment a man starts loving his secretary as if she were his wife, something goes seriously wrong.[26] A love is still there between these, but it is a disordered love that is not able to lead them to their final end.

We may ask why for Dante Francesca and Paolo are found in hell. The two were friends but Francesca was married to Paolo's brother. At one point passion for each other seized them and they committed adultery with each other. Found by Francesca's husband, they were both slain in the very act. Dante finds them swept together by the wind on the second terrace of hell and seeks to question them about what had happened, upon which Francesca responds:

> Love, which soon seizes on a well-born heart,
>
> seized him for that fair body's sake, whereof

---

circumstances. The urgent need to look after someone who is wounded can make other things that could be done secondary, for example, spending time with one's wife, but this does not mean that a man loves the wounded person more than his wife."

25. See Melina, *Epiphany of Love*, 38: "If our ultimate and formal intentionality is directed to the person of the other, it passes through the choice of what is truly good for that person. The good of a particular action, which our will chooses from the perspective of communion, has an objective weight, independent of the subject, which must be verified by reason as to its capacity to effectively promote the good of the person of the other. The guarantee that this is an authentic love of friendship . . . is given by the will's submission to the truth about good."

26. See Noriega, "Love and Reason."

> I was deprived; and still the way offends me.
>
> Love, which absolves from loving none that's loved,
>
> seized me so strongly for his love of me,
>
> that, as thou see'st, it doth not leave me yet.
>
> Love to a death in common led us on;
>
> Cain's ice awaiteth him who quenched our life.[27]

The affirmation Dante makes here is fearful and tremendous: There are loves that bring us to hell. Francesca and Paolo were friends, even good friends; however they sought other goods over and above those involved in a mere friendship, and thus their love became disordered, leading them away and excluding them from God, their final end.

Thus, the question is urgent: how do we order our loves well? Order implies the disposition or arrangement towards an end. The ultimate end of human life is communion and friendship with God and, in God, with all other friends of God. To be rightly ordered, our loves must be ordered towards this end. The *ordo amoris* ultimately means well-ordered, harmonious relationships. But how are our relationships well-ordered? Before ordering our acts, which take the form of a response, human reason finds an order in the reality of the things themselves. There is a *logos* that is inherent to being a father, a husband, a wife, a colleague, a fellow-traveler. Our friendships and relationships have their own *ratio*, their own *logos* that is inherent to them, an intelligibility that reason finds the moment it opens itself to reality.

In fact, it was not that Francesca and Paolo were mistaken about what is implied in being a good wife or husband but rather that they did not keep the love to which they had already committed before their eyes, i.e., in Francesca's case: the love for her husband. This is where the demanding element of our response comes in. We have to remain attentive to the reality of our relationships and of our loves as they are given. We must not close our eyes and we must not forget. We constantly have to keep our true loves painted before our eyes so as not to be swept away in a moment of temptation. We are reminded of St. Paul's strong admonition to the Galatians: "O you foolish Galatians! Who has bewitched you, before whose eyes was painted Jesus Christ as crucified?" What is the main problem here? Christ was painted before their eyes, but they have taken their eyes off of Jesus. They stopped looking at him and wandered astray.

27. Dante, *Divine Comedy I, Inferno*, V, 100–107.

To order our loves, we must look at our beloved. In fact, we are responsible for forgetting, even though we never chose to forget. We are responsible for forgetting because we did not choose to take the necessary measures to remind ourselves. That is where the problem is. We can fail to consider a reality and in this way avoid being touched by it. In its beginning, love is the encounter with the concrete reality of the other; it is an encounter that gives me the promise of fulfillment.[28] In this very beginning there is already contained the principle or *logos* that defines the kind of love and that defines the kind of relationship. My freedom comes in as I respond to this encounter, as I respond to this reality that first touched me. To respond adequately, I have to open my eyes and allow the reality of the other to become real to me. In this way, I will become aware of what it means for the other to be my spouse, my mother, my father, my brother, my friend, or a stranger in need of my help. Only when we discover the order that is intrinsic to these relationships can we order our response well. But to find this order, we must be attentive to what reality has to say. The reality of the other invites me to communion, not with an abstract humanity but with the concrete reality of individual persons, according to an order inherent to the relationships as they are given.

What, then, is the relationship between the universal and the concrete? Turning around the words of the old physician with which we started, we may in fact be amazed at ourselves: the more we love people in particular, that is, individually, as separate persons the more we will love humankind in general, since, in fact, it is precisely in individual men and women that we encounter humanity.

28. See Melina, "Love," 16–28.

7

Building the Kingdom on Earth?

Evangelical Zeal and the Utopian Temptation

Perfect Systems?

TOWARD THE BEGINNING OF his "Choruses from 'The Rock,'" T. S. Eliot asks himself why people would love the church. He points out that it could not be on account of her telling them what they want to hear. She reminds them of unpleasant facts having to do with life and death, sin and evil, which they would prefer not to hear. Her judgment is curiously opposed to theirs. Where she is soft, they are hard and the other way around. While the church speaks to people of reality, they would much rather flee into a dream world, imagining forms of social organization whose structures are so perfect that individuals will be exempted from having to be good.[1]

What is it about the church that would make people love her? What is the church's mission? It cannot be other than the mission of her Lord: to proclaim the kingdom of God, for this is why, according to his own testimony, Christ had come: "I must preach the good news of the kingdom of God to the other cities also; for I was sent for this purpose" (Luke 4:43). In what follows, we will reflect on what proclaiming the kingdom of God means and what it does not mean. We will ask whether the primary goal of this mission is to make the world a better place, i.e., to contribute to

---

1. See Eliot, "Choruses from 'The Rock,'" 159.

earthly social progress, or whether it is to help people to become better, i.e., to call them to conversion. These two goals are certainly not exclusive of each other, and yet there would seem to be a hierarchy. Pope Francis points out in *Evangelii Gaudium*, "it is imperative to evangelize cultures in order to inculturate the Gospel."[2] In what follows, we will reflect on how this can best be done.

According to Eliot, we may say that the church's mission, her way of proclaiming the kingdom, is to remind people of the ultimate realities, of the gift of life and the fact of death. It is to apply a judgment that is different from the judgment of the world, since it applies a different standard. The church is not afraid of speaking about evil and sin, calling it by name, while people would rather ignore these disagreeable truths. She would seem to be interested in helping people to be good rather than in helping them to create systems so perfectly organized that they are exonerated from having to be good.

What the American-British poet may have had in mind here are systems of the like described by Thomas Hobbes or Immanuel Kant. For Hobbes, people are originally enemies of one another. By creating a State and delegating some of their powers to it, they render social living somewhat tolerable.[3] Kant can imagine a republic of devils in which the laws are so perfect that its demonic citizens, by strictly pursuing their own self-interests and without harboring an ounce of good-will for their fellow devils, promote the common good at the same time.[4]

But perhaps Eliot refers to yet another current of thought, such as Marxist ideology. For Marx, human persons are entirely the product of

---

2. Francis, *Evangelii Gaudium*, no. 69.

3. See Hobbes, *Leviathan*, Part II, Chapter 17, 111: "The final cause, end, or design of men, (who naturally love liberty, and dominion over others,) in the introduction of that restraint upon themselves, (in which we see them live in commonwealths,) is the foresight of their own preservation, and of a more contented life thereby; that is to say, of getting themselves out from that miserable condition of war, which is necessarily consequent . . . to the natural passions of men, when there is no visible power to keep them in awe, and tie them by fear of punishment to the performance of their covenants."

4. See Kant, *To Perpetual Peace*, 23. "The problem of organizing a nation is solvable even for a people comprised of devils (if only they possess understanding). The problem can be stated in this way: 'So order and organize a group of rational beings who require universal laws for their preservation—though each is secretly inclined to exempt himself from such laws—that, while their private attitudes conflict, these nonetheless so cancel one another that these beings behave publicly just as if they had no evil attitudes.' This kind of problem must be *solvable*" (original emphasis).

their surrounding social structures.[5] If they commit evil deeds, they do so because they experience want and need. Highly confident in the newly-unleashed powers of industry, Marx thought that by arranging for the public ownership of the means of production, one could create a society of superabundance, where no one would ever experience any lack of anything. The remedy of all social evil is the Communist Revolution, on the other side of which one would have a society where everyone gives "according to his abilities" and receives "according to his need."[6] As we mentioned in the previous chapter, Robert Spaemann emphasizes that the point here is not so much to create a just society, but rather to create a society in which justice will no longer be necessary—simply because all goods are available in superabundance.[7] Marxism indeed dreamed of a system so perfect that no one needs to be good. No one would ever have to consider giving to others their due, simply because all things human beings could ever want are to be had in superabundance. Whether such systems are even thinkable may be an open question, but there is no doubt that the communist experiment has failed at an extremely high human cost. T.S. Eliot's premonition has certainly proven true: human beings as they are in reality will win the day over human beings as wishful thinking has them.[8] And in any case, he is suggesting that it could not possibly the church's task to assist people in coming up with such systems; it is her task to call people to convert to the good, not to make goodness unnecessary.

Earthly Progress and the Kingdom of God

In its pastoral constitution *Gaudium et Spes* the Second Vatican Council declares: "Although we must be careful to distinguish earthly progress clearly from the increase of the kingdom of Christ, such progress is of vital concern

5. We are following here the interpretation of Marxist utopianism given by Jonas, *Imperative of Responsibility*, 158: "Man is basically 'good' and only made bad by circumstances. All that is therefore needed for his essential goodness to become actual are the proper circumstances. Or, what comes practically to the same, man—with *no* determinate essence—is the product of circumstances, and good circumstances will produce good men. . . . Only the classless society will bring with it the good man. This is the 'utopia' in the essence of Marxism" (original emphasis).

6. Marx, *Critique of the Gotha Programme*, 321; see Jonas, *Imperative of Responsibility*, 194.

7. See Spaemann, *Basic Moral Concepts*, 36–37.

8. See Eliot, "Choruses from 'The Rock,'" 159.

to the kingdom of God, insofar as it can contribute to the better ordering of human society."[9] What is the Council saying here? The thought contained in the main phrase, and hence presumably the central idea of the sentence, is that earthly progress and a good social order are of great interest to the kingdom of God. The idea contained in the subordinate clause might easily be overlooked due to its syntactical position. However, it would also seem relevant, if only as an important qualification meant to prevent the reader from misinterpreting the intention of the Council fathers: earthly progress and the increase of God's kingdom are not the same thing.

Undoubtedly there are some particularly dark times in history, where the kingdom suffers violence, where the seeds of God's truth are suffocated by weeds, devoured by the birds or dried up by the sun, times in which it is particularly difficult for the kingdom to grow and for human beings to be good. Thus Hannah Arendt, reflecting on Adolf Eichmann's life story, surmises that "under more favorable circumstances, it is highly unlikely" that this great administrator of the Holocaust would have come before the court in Jerusalem "or any other criminal court."[10] To her mind, in any case, he would have certainly not become one of the greatest criminals of the period. It is probably never easy to be good and most likely this side of heaven the kingdom will always encounter the resistance of the human heart. And yet, there are times and places and social arrangements that make it particularly hard to be good and that offer resistance to God's reign that is quite out of the ordinary. Hence it is certainly true that a good social order can contribute to the increase of the kingdom, as *Gaudium et Spes* suggests. But perhaps today, in our age of new ideologies that offer previously unheard of content for what a kingdom of God on earth might look like (not a classless, but a sexless, gender-mainstreamed society), we do well not to forget the subordinate clause: "We must be careful to distinguish earthly progress clearly from the increase of the kingdom of Christ."[11]

The fact is that in the New Testament, the kingdom of heaven is never said to be the product of human progress or construction. There are certainly laborers in the vineyard (Matt 20:1–16) but a vineyard is cultivated like a garden, not built like a house. The vines grow by themselves, as does the grain of the field. When Jesus speaks of the kingdom, we learn that it "comes" (Matt 6:10; Luke 10:9), that it needs to be "received" (Luke 18:17),

9. Second Vatican Council, *Gaudium et Spes*, no. 39.

10. Arendt, *Eichmann in Jerusalem*, 278–79.

11. Second Vatican Council, *Gaudium et Spes*, no. 39.

that it "is in the midst" of us (Luke 17:21)—and yet that it is "not of this world" (John 18:36). It is *never* the work of human hands.[12] The German historian Leopold von Ranke suggests that "every epoch is immediate to God, and that its value in no way depends on what may have eventuated from it, but rather in its existence alone, its own unique particularity."[13] With this, he is evidently entering into polemics against Hegel, for whom History is the process in which the World Spirit becomes increasingly conscious of itself. On this account, each previous period in history is but a function of the later ones. But of course von Ranke is also already anticipating a response to Marx, who replaces Hegel's World Spirit with the Revolution as the earthly *eschaton* that brings History to its fulfillment and deprives all that was prior of its significance. The same Apostle who by saying that "salvation is nearer to us now than when we first believed" (Rom 13:11) likewise apparently suggests a dynamic understanding of history as a process of growth toward a final point, also insists that "we who are alive, who are left until the coming of the Lord, shall not precede those who have fallen asleep" (1 Thess 4:15), not having any advantage over them.

God's kingdom—his salvific action—has broken into human history, it manifests itself in human history, and it is offered to us in human history. Yet, welcoming the kingdom of heaven does not mean bringing human history to its fulfillment by our efforts. By placing the point of fulfillment of human history *within* human history, the utopian ideologies of the last century have committed the most lethal mistake known to human history, ultimately drenching the earth with the blood of millions: if human history is fulfilled in a future that is within history, then the present is devalued for this future to the point of sacrificing or at least risking present humanity for a future one that is allegedly enhanced or more authentic. In short utopianism is characterized by what Hans Jonas calls "the ontology of 'not yet.'"[14] The present epoch, with all its ambiguity and tentativeness, is seen

12. See Melina, *Epiphany of Love*, 129: "It is absolutely clear that the kingdom of God is not the fruit of human action. Human action can in no way claim to bring about what is a pure transcendental gift, what surpasses every creaturely possibility."

13. von Ranke, *Secret of World History*, 159.

14. See Jonas, *Imperative of Responsibility*, 200. Jonas himself, however, does not entirely stay clear of the utopian temptation when he posits the survival of humanity as absolute earthly good for the sake of which one could suspend any moral concerns, at least temporarily: "Averting disaster takes precedence over everything else, including pursuit of the good, and suspends otherwise inviolable prohibitions and rule" ("Toward a Philosophy of Technology," 43). For a further examination of this problem see Kampowski, *Greater Freedom*, 112–17.

as a mere function of a future one, where human history, and with this, humanity, will finally come to its true being.

To move to this final stage, i.e., to build the kingdom of God immanent to human history, human efforts are said to be needed. These efforts are guided by whatever idea one has of this kingdom: a post-revolutionary classless society of material superabundance; a world ruled by a pure Arian race; a world in which war has finally been abolished thanks to the benefits of biotechnological engineering, which has pacified people, liberating them of all unsettling passions like love, hate or fear.[15] However this earthly kingdom of God will be defined, it is by definition not a kingdom that *comes* but one that is *made*. This *making* implies violence, which, according to Marx, is the midwife of history.[16] All things are permitted to the one who knows the final point of history, as Lenin and his followers clearly saw.[17]

It is from history's point of fulfillment that words like "good" and "bad" then receive their meaning. Within a Marxist context, "good" becomes synonymous with "that which leads up to the Revolution" and "bad" is "that which obstructs the revolution." If impoverishing the working classes paves the way to the Revolution, then impoverishing the working classes is a good thing.[18] If purging the world of capitalists serves the Revolution, then shedding their blood is a good thing. After all, you cannot make an omelet without breaking eggs. And yet, it has become time for the eggs to speak up,

15. See Huxley, *Brave New World*.

16. See Marx, *Capital*, vol. 1, 916: "Force is the midwife of every old society which is pregnant with a new one." The German word *Gewalt*, which is rendered here with "force," is more aptly translated as "violence" in this context.

17. See Shub, *Lenin: A Biography*, 368, citing from the Bolshevik publication *Red Sword* (August 18, 1919): "Ours is a new morality. Our humanism is absolute, for it has as its basis the desire for the abolition of all oppression and tyranny. To us everything is permitted."

18. See once more Pope Benedict XVI's criticism of the Marxist theory of impoverishment, which we have already referred to in the previous chapter. According to Marx, in order to create a future authentic humanity, one should precisely *not* offer any assistance to the working poor, which would only serve to prolong unjust social structures. Rather, the aim should be that, under the pressure of poverty, there will finally be a revolution which will cause these unjust structures to collapse. This is indeed one of the ways in which utopia sacrifices present humanity to the future one. In response Benedict argues, "Seen in this way, charity is rejected and attacked as a means of preserving the *status quo*. What we have here, though, is really an inhuman philosophy. People of the present are sacrificed to the *moloch* of the future—a future whose effective realization is at best doubtful. One does not make the world more human by refusing to act humanely here and now" (*Deus Caritas Est*, no. 31).

as Hannah Arendt put it.[19] After witnessing the murderous consequences of the two totalitarian regimes of the twentieth century, of Nazism and Stalinism, we must utterly resist the temptation to make omelets. Or, to revert back from metaphor to plain speech: we must resist the temptation to look at the kingdom of God as something to be created by human hands. Looking at the kingdom in this way would mean to devalue the present epoch and with it the people who live in it. Present humanity could be sacrificed in order to move history to its final point, from which alone history would receive its meaning. To repeat von Ranke's invaluable insight: "Each epoch is immediate to God and its value does not consist in what originates from it, but in its own existence." Or, again, to say it with *Gaudium et Spes*, "We must be careful to distinguish earthly progress clearly from the increase of the kingdom of Christ."

Where the Kingdom Is Revealed

Thus, the first danger with identifying the kingdom of heaven and social progress lies in a utopianism that aims at bringing history to its fulfillment in time, that is, to say, "Social progress is like the kingdom of God." Some kind of social achievement or ideal, such as the classless society, is set as an absolute from which everything else is judged. But then, there may also be the inverse problem, essentially saying, "The kingdom of God is like social progress," interpreting the absolute demands that the kingdom has on us as if they were nothing but social policies of human law. It is true, after all, that the kingdom does lay unconditional claims upon Christ's disciples that are indeed relevant for this life on earth. Thus, Our Lord says, "No one who puts his hand to the plow and looks back is fit for the kingdom of God" (Luke 9:62). And the Apostle reminds the believers in Corinth that "neither the immoral, nor idolaters, nor adulterers, nor sexual perverts, nor thieves, nor the greedy, nor drunkards, nor revilers, nor robbers will inherit the kingdom of God" (1 Cor 6:9–10). The kingdom is in the tension between the "already" and the "not yet." Inasmuch as it is "not yet," it is the fulfillment of history that transcends history. Insofar as it is "already," it is "in our midst" and has concrete repercussions for our lives. In the preaching of Jesus we see how the proclamation of the kingdom goes hand in hand with a call to conversion (*metanoia*) (see Mark 1:15) that implies a radical change in behavior (see John 8:11).

19. See Arendt, "Eggs Speak Up," 270–84.

The growth of the kingdom cannot be measured in terms of the growth of earthly social structures or technological abilities. While social and cultural circumstances can indeed make it difficult for people to receive the kingdom, it is nonetheless true that even in the historically darkest hours the kingdom breaks in. Where was the kingdom at the time of the Diocletian persecution, the last and the most violent persecution Christians had to suffer at the hands of the Roman Empire? The kingdom was there in the believers' willingly surrendering their lives for their faith, in the very blood they shed. It was there in the pagans, who protected and defended their Christian friends. It was there even in those who succumbed to the threat of violence, failing their Lord and Savior and who later repented and were generously readmitted to the church of Christ. It shines forth in all those single acts of courage, faithfulness, and forgiveness, that indeed by their very being make the world a better place. To say it with Robert Spaemann, "Actions are not good or bad by virtue of the fact that they improve or worsen the world; rather, they improve or worsen the world because they are good or bad."[20]

The absolute claims of the kingdom are not about an ideal state to be brought about in the future, but about a concrete way of life to be lived in the here and now in response to God's grace. The early church was quite aware of the fact that it was something about the way Christians lived that distinguished them from all others. In the second-century *Epistle to Diognetus* we read:

> The difference between Christians and the rest of mankind is not a matter of nationality, or language, or custom. . . . They pass their lives in whatever township . . . and conform to ordinary local usage in their clothing, diet, and other habits. Nevertheless, the organization of their community does exhibit some features that are remarkable, and even surprising. For instance, though they are residents at home in their own countries, their behavior there is more like that of transients. . . . Like all men, they marry and beget children, though they do not expose their infants. Any Christian is free to share his neighbor's table, but never his marriage bed. Though destiny has placed them here in the flesh, they do not live after the flesh; their days are passed on earth, but their citizenship is above in the heavens.[21]

---

20. Spaemann, "Individual Actions," 152.

21. *Epistle to Diognetus*, in *Early Christian Writings*, 144–45.

The believers' citizenship is in heaven and yet, it has concrete repercussions on the way they live their lives on earth. And while in general customs Christians are essentially indistinguishable from people of their surrounding culture—in today's terms we may say they wear the same clothes, watch the same movies, drive the same cars—they are nonetheless distinguished precisely by their moral behavior, for instance, they do not commit adultery or practice what today we would call abortion.

Identifying the kingdom with social progress may lead us to lose sight of the absolute claims that the kingdom makes on our lives, which are then no longer seen as unconditional but are understood to be as relative as any non-utopian claims to social progress will necessarily have to be. Faithfulness in marriage and unconditional respect for the life of every human being—including the unborn, the less-abled, the weak, the dying—may no longer be seen as a manifestation and anticipation of the kingdom of heaven, an unconditional requirement for anyone wanting to live "the kingdom-way," but rather as some political option among others. Pope Francis points out how "the predominant school of thought sometimes leads to 'false compassion' which holds that it is a benefit to women to promote abortion; an act of dignity to perform euthanasia," so that we are living in what he deplores as a "throw-away culture."[22] Indeed, in modern states everything becomes negotiable; questions regarding divorce and remarriage, abortion and euthanasia are treated as if they were similar to problems of tax laws. We are guided by our own little lights; there is nothing intrinsically right or wrong, just more or less expedient. Hence, everything is debatable; there are no more moral absolutes in politics to guide legislation.

This kind of thinking, at times for explicit fear of utopianism, tends to deny all truth and deems no good worthy of unconditional protection.[23] Given that rendering absolute some earthly goal has had disastrous effects, relativism now becomes the new humanism, while whoever speaks of nonnegotiable moral truths that have their ultimate foundation in God is at times publically associated with the murderers of the Third Reich.[24] The intolerance

22. Francis, "Address to Participants in the Commemorative Conference of the Italian Catholic Physicians' Association."

23. For an extremely polemical, though not unintelligent, apology for relativism in politics: Flores d'Arcais, "La democrazia."

24. See ibid., 42–43: "If I advance my own values as God's decree, I turn every conflict into an interminable battle among gods, transforming every dissent into inextinguishable theological hatred. Every political decision becomes a trial by ordeal, a judgment of God. . . . If we admit God's will in the democratic gathering place, we will

of the self-confessed "liberals" has already been decried by Leo XIII at the end of the nineteenth century.[25] It is not a new phenomenon that those who claim to advance the cause of tolerance are the most intolerant when it comes to dealing with people who do not share their opinions.[26]

Yet every error has some truth to it; otherwise it would have no appeals and would not spread. In the sphere of politics and social progress, many things are indeed debatable. It is the sphere where divergent, even contrary, opinions can all be legitimate. But for there to be a meaningful debate, it would seem that some issues should not and could not be put into question, inasmuch as they are the very conditions for the possibility of there being questions in the first place. Hannah Arendt gives a simple example to distinguish these two kinds of issues: while it may be "an open question where it is better to put [. . . a] bridge,"—a matter that "can be decided . . . by debate"—"there shouldn't be any debate about the question that everybody should have decent housing"[27]—as if that were any doubt about that. Politicians can legitimately argue and disagree on what is the just course of action under given conditions; they can debate on what is the best way of expressing in terms of law the recognition that is due to each human being. They must *not* discuss whether to enact just laws or rather unjust ones, whether to recognize each human being's dignity before the law or rather to exclude certain categories of human beings from legal protection. To the extent that they do so, they place themselves outside the context of law and civility. After all, law is by definition concerned with justice, and civility by

---

in the end find ourselves with all the same possible secular unrest, but now expanded beyond measure as everyone who can call himself Benjamin will seek to legitimize his delusions of omnipotence. In Hebrew, Benjamin means 'God with us.' But the 'Gott mit uns' has resounded too recently, in a holocaust of too many Benjamins, for us to forget the abysses into which the obstinacy of proclaiming God's name in public life can cast *homo sapiens*" (my own translation).

25. Leo XIII, *Libertas Praestantissimum*, no. 35: "And as to *tolerance*, it is surprising how far removed from the equity and prudence of the Church are those who profess what is called liberalism. . . . And because the Church . . . is forced utterly to reprobate and condemn tolerance of such an abandoned and criminal character, they calumniate her as being wanting in patience and gentleness. . . . But, in spite of all this show of tolerance, it very often happens that, while they profess themselves ready to lavish liberty on all in the greatest profusion, they are utterly intolerant toward the Catholic Church, by refusing to allow her the liberty of being herself free" (original emphasis).

26. See Flores d'Arcais, "*La democrazia*," 118: "[Relativism] thus demands and prohibits according to a common ethos that is intolerant only with the intolerant" (my own translation).

27. Arendt, "On Hannah Arendt," 317–18.

its very notion includes the recognition of others as having the same dignity as oneself. Those who put into question the bases of law and civility do not act as politicians but as gangsters. These questions are not political ones and even to raise them is to be immoral.[28]

The reason people find it increasingly difficult to see the difference between political issues on the one hand and moral or immoral ones on the other is the rise of legal positivism that reduces morality to legality and legality to conformity with the will of the legislator. There is no action that is in itself good or bad, moral or immoral. There are only actions that are in conformity with human positive law or not. Evidently, on this account of morality and law, none of the Nazi murderers should have ever been sentenced in the Nuremberg trials, given that they had acted on Hitler's command, which in Germany at the time had the force of law.[29] If we do not consider the Nuremberg trials an instance of the victors lording it over the vanquished, then it is only because we take recourse to the same criterion as did the judges back then: our common humanity, which is not the result of legality but rather that which makes legality possible in the first place.

The Church and the Kingdom: Changing Structures or Calling to Conversion?

What would happen if the absolute claims of the kingdom were not only ignored or looked upon with suspicion by secular society but even by some representatives of the church? What would happen if moral relativism and legal positivism were to enter into her bosom under the pretext of improving her as if she were a society like any other? She would find it hard to preach conversion but rather seek to find solutions to problems by changing legislations and structures, as any secular human authority would do. Hence, it is rather worrisome that in the current synodal debate on the family at times one gets the impression that the moral question of the spouses' mutual fidelity is reduced to a question of canon law, and canon law itself is interpreted in a positivistic way. These tendencies may, after all, be symptoms of an

---

28. Thus, Aristotle observes that not every question should be treated. A question can itself be immoral, so that some people do not need instruction, but rather punishment and correction: "For those who feel doubt whether or not the gods ought to be honoured and parents loved, need castigation" (*Topica*, I, 11, 105a).

29. See Arendt, *Eichmann in Jerusalem*, 148.

understanding of God's kingdom in terms of relative earthly progress and of the church in terms of any other human society.

Thus we need to ask about the church's relation to the kingdom. The church is of course a visible society with hierarchical structures, and in this she is not dissimilar to other human institutions. But she is also the Mystical body of Christ. She is characterized by a human and a divine element, which, according to *Lumen Gentium*, "are not to be thought of as two realities. On the contrary, they form one complete reality. . . . For this reason the Church is compared, not without significance, to the mystery of the incarnate Word."[30] She is "the kingdom of Christ already present in mystery,"[31] sharing in the threefold office of Christ as prophet, priest, and king. All this means that, although she is a society, we cannot quite apply the same logic to her governance as to the governance of secular society. Human law can serve the kingdom, sometimes for better, sometimes for worse, but the logic proper to human law cannot be the logic to guide the church. For instance, a human legislator may rightly see it fit to tolerate certain evils in secular society, but the church cannot simply tolerate her faithful's evil deeds. Rather she is calling to conversion. Because of the mission she has from God, she calls sin by its name, and because of the love she bears for sinners, she exhorts them to change their ways.

Tolerance is indifferent to the fate of others. In this sense it is much opposed to true mercy that takes interest in them and wants their true good. The sinners' true good is that they convert and come to embrace the way of life that is truly fulfilling—even this side of heaven. Hence, inasmuch as she is a loving mother, the church is not indifferent to us; she cannot tolerate our evil acts but opens up for us the path of penitence that is the path of changing our behavior. Indeed, the hopeful conviction that by the grace of God people are in fact able to change their ways and their thinking (*metanoia*) is what the church has received from her Founder: "The kingdom of God is at hand; repent, and believe in the gospel" (Mark 1:15).

---

30. Second Vatican Council, *Lumen Gentium*, no. 8. The document continues in the same number: "As the assumed nature, inseparably united to him, serves the divine Word as a living organ of salvation, so, in a somewhat similar way, does the social structure of the Church serve the Spirit of Christ who vivifies it, in the building up of the body (see Eph. 4:15)."

31. Ibid., no. 3.

8

Love of the Common Good: The Principle of Social Life

Love and Social Life: An Antagonism?

"THE PROBLEM OF ORGANIZING a nation is solvable even for a people comprised of devils (if only they possess understanding)."[1] This is Immanuel Kant's provocative thesis, and it may serve as a very good summary of the modern attitude. For modernity, building a working commonwealth is not a question of morality, and goodwill has little to do with it. It is simply a matter of intelligence, of inventing a clever arrangement in which each person by egoistically pursuing his or her own aims happens to work for the good of all. This indeed would seem to be something of which even the devils are in principle capable. In this sense Kant continues:

> The problem can be stated in this way: "So order and organize a group of rational beings who require universal laws for their preservation—though each is secretly inclined to exempt himself from such laws—that, while their private attitudes conflict, these nonetheless so cancel one another that these beings behave publicly just as if they had no evil attitudes." This kind of problem must be *solvable*.[2]

It is clear that in such a conceptual framework, love does not play any role inasmuch as love is simply unnecessary. For Kant, in an intelligently

1. Kant, *To Perpetual Peace*, 23.
2. Ibid. (original emphasis).

organized commonwealth, no good-will of the citizens for each other is needed. In fact, love may even be a hindrance. Thus, when John Rawls proposes that people deliberating about the procedural principles of justice put on a veil of ignorance, so as to find themselves in what he calls the "original position,"[3] what he implies is not only that they do not know which place they will occupy in the society they are shaping by their laws, i.e., they do not know whether they will be kings or pawns—no, the veil of ignorance also covers any preferential relation, which may otherwise compromise the impartiality of one's judgment. It is certainly not without reason that, when personified in art, the virtue of justice is usually portrayed blindfolded, holding a scale in her hands and meting out impartial judgment. For modernity, justice is identified as the constitutive virtue of a commonwealth. It is said to exclude any preference and hence love, inasmuch as love is a preferential and somewhat interested relationship.

What is at stake here is of course a certain vision of the human being and his or her relation to society. As Emmanuel Levinas formulates it, society may in fact be understood as "the result of a limitation of the principle that men are predators of one another." In this case, "the social, with its institutions, universal forms and laws" would be conceived as resulting "from limiting the consequences of the war between men." An alternative way of looking at society is to conceive it as resulting "from the limitation of the principle that men are *for* one another," i.e., "from limiting the infinity which opens in the ethical relationship of man to man."[4] Levinas certainly opts for the second way: society for him is the mode in which the infinite responsibility that human beings have for each other is structured and delimited, introducing what in traditional terms has been called an *ordo amoris*, an order of love or of responsibility, into the interpersonal relationships among human beings.[5]

3. Rawls, *Theory of Justice*, 136–37: "The idea of the original position is to set up a fair procedure so that any principles agreed to will be just. The aim is to use the notion of pure procedural justice as a basis of the theory. Somehow we must nullify the effects of specific contingencies which put men at odds and tempt them to exploit social and natural circumstances to their own advantage. Now in order to do this I assume that the parties are situated behind a veil of ignorance. They do not know how the various alternatives will affect their own particular case and they are obliged to evaluate principles solely on the basis of general considerations."

4. Levinas, *Ethics and Infinity*, 80 (original emphasis).

5. See for instance Spaemann, *Happiness and Benevolence*, 106–18.

Modernity, in contrast, has for the most part followed the first option formulated by Levinas: *homo homini lupus*, man is a wolf to man, as Thomas Hobbes has it, taking up the ancient Roman poet Plautus.[6] Human beings, in other words, will naturally devour each other unless law intervenes, cleverly using their egoistic tendencies in order to build social structures that are in the interest of all. Thus, for Hobbes governments exist simply due to the citizens' fear of violent death and their desire for ease.[7] Adam Smith concurs in essentially seeing fear as the fundamental motive of why people live in an ordered society ruled by law, namely the fear for their property. For him, the only legitimate function of government is "the defence of the rich against the poor, or of those who have some property against those who have none at all."[8] If all this is true, i.e., if human beings are truly this way, i.e., if they are essentially wild animals endowed with cunning, and if the sole purpose of society is to mitigate the effects of human egoism by turning those tendencies—quite against their nature—to the use of the public good, then it seems that Kant is right and that in principle also the devils should be able to build such a commonwealth, the whole purpose of which then would be indeed, as Hannah Arendt suggests, nothing but the common wealth.[9]

The human person, on this view, is an essentially isolated, private individual who proceeds from desire to desire[10] but never advances a step beyond himself,[11] accidentally united to others through economic exchange but ultimately in competition with them for scarce private goods. "The whole philosophy of Hell"—the devil Screwtape instructs his apprentice Wormwood in C.S. Lewis's famous *Screwtape Letters*—"rests on recognition of the axiom that one thing is not another thing, and, specially, that one self is not another self. My good is my good and your good is yours. What one gains another loses. Even an inanimate object is what it is by

6. Hobbes, *Man and Citizen: De Homine and De Cive*, 89: "To speak impartially, both sayings are very true: that man to man is a kind of God; and that man to man is an arrant wolf. The first is true, if we compare citizens amongst themselves; and the second, if we compare cities." (See Plautus, *Asinaria*, 495: "Lupus est homo homini.")

7. See Hobbes, *Leviathan,* Part I, Chapter XI, 66: "Desire of ease, and sensual delight, disposeth men to obey a common power: . . . Fear of death, and wounds, disposeth to the same." See also Hobbes, *Leviathan,* Part II, Chapter XX, 132.

8. Smith, *Wealth of Nations*, Book V, Chapter 1, 465.

9. See Arendt, *Human Condition*, 68.

10. See Hobbes, *Leviathan*, Part I, Chapter XI, 66.

11. See Hume, *Treatise of Human Nature,* Book I, Part 2, Section 6, 49.

excluding all other objects from the space it occupies; if it expands, it does so by thrusting other objects aside or by absorbing them. A self does the same. . . . 'To be' means 'to be in competition.'"[12]

Challenging the Antagonism Between
Love and Social Life

This philosophy of course can and must be challenged. To challenge this conception we need to ask about the human person's true good. What is his or her true interest? Let us take a brief look at Aristotle's definitions of the human being. The Philosopher is often said to have defined the human being as a rational animal and as a social animal. These ways of rendering Aristotle's original Greek, though perhaps not entirely incorrect, may nonetheless be slightly misleading. "Rational animal" may make one think simply of a living being capable of "reckoning with consequences" to say it with Hobbes,[13] or of a particularly clever beast, as Friedrich Nietzsche has it.[14] "Social animal" may simply suggest some kind of gregarious character as it occurs also in animals such as ants, bees, or wolves. What Aristotle in fact says is that the human being alone of all the animals possesses *logos*, the word, or language.[15] It is of course true that *logos* can also denote reason, rationality, or meaning, but these, for Aristotle, are most closely related to language. For him, to be rational precisely means to have the word. The context, too, makes it clear that in the passage from the *Politics* under discussion one has to translate *logos* with "language" or "word." In the phrases that immediately follow, Aristotle explains that it is by the *logos* that human beings communicate about what is right and wrong, or just and unjust, moral or immoral. Given that nature does nothing in vain, and given that nature has given human beings the word, Aristotle argues that they are *political* animals and not just gregarious. They alone have perception of the good and the bad, and it is by their communication about these

---

12. Lewis, *Screwtape Letters*, 94.

13. See Hobbes, *Leviathan*, Part I, Chapter V, 28: "Out of all which we may define, (that is to say determine,) what that is which is meant by this word *reason*, when we reckon it amongst the faculties of the mind. For reason, in this sense, is nothing but *reckoning* (that is adding and subtracting) of the consequences of general names agreed upon, for the *marking* and *signifying* of our thoughts" (original emphases).

14. See Nietzsche, "On Truth and Lies," 114.

15. Aristotle, *Politics*, I, 1, 1253a10.

things—which takes place by means of language—that the household and city are built.[16] In other words, human persons are political animals because they are living beings who have the word, living beings that have language, which goes beyond mere reckoning with consequences; they are not just particularly clever beasts.

That human beings are defined by the word or by language means that they are defined by relationships, as the word is something they necessarily have to receive. We cannot give the word to ourselves; we need to receive it from others. The word implies an interlocutor; it implies an original being-placed-in-relationship. This is what Vladimir Solovyov convincingly points out when he writes,

> Social life is not a condition superadded to the individual life, but is contained in the very definition of personality which is essentially a rationally-knowing and a morally-active force—both knowing and acting being possible only in the life of a community. Rational knowledge on its *formal* side is conditioned by *general notions* which express a unity of meaning in an endless multiplicity of events; the real and objective universality (the general meaning) of notions manifests itself in language as a means of communication, without which rational activity cannot develop, and, for lack of realization, gradually disappears altogether or becomes merely potential. Language—this concrete reason—could not have been the work of an isolated individual, and consequently such an individual could not be rational, could not be human.[17]

From the fact, then, that human beings have the word, it follows that they are political beings. This means that they are most fully themselves, actualizing what they are in the most perfect degree, when they live in a *polis* or city, i.e., in a form of living together structured by law and mutual promises.[18] Explaining what he means by "nature," Aristotle says that it "is

16. See ibid., I, 1, 1253a10–19: "And why man is a political animal in a greater measure than any bee or any gregarious animal is clear. For nature, as we declare, does nothing without purpose; and man alone of the animals possesses speech. . . . Speech is designed to indicate the advantageous and the harmful, and therefore also the right and the wrong; for it is the special property of man in distinction from the other animals that he alone has perception of good and bad and right and wrong and the other moral qualities, and it is partnership in these things that makes a household and a city-state."

17. Solovyov, *Justification of the Good*, 175 (original emphases).

18. See Spaemann, *Zur Kritik der politischen Utopie*, 186: "[The] Aristotelean thesis says . . . not only that in order to be themselves, human beings need reliable protection from one another. Rather, it says that the human being can become a self and realize the

an end," namely "that which each thing is when its growth is completed" and then continues to say "the city is of nature."[19] Man is naturally a city-building being, i.e., he is naturally a cultural being, and the foundation of culture is found in language.

Like any living being, human beings live their lives in the tension between mere life and the good life. To live well as a human being means to live in community, and not just in the sense of living next to one another, but in a community, structured by law, by mutual promises, by covenants, that is, in a *polis*. The city "exists for the good life," Aristotle points out.[20] Human beings do not just reckon with consequences. They have the word, they have language by which they can enter into relation with others. The human being who has the word, we may say, has the word in order to give the word.

In many languages "to give one's word" means precisely to promise, to enter into covenant with others. The human being, the political animal who has the word, is a being made for the covenant. If this is how things are, then we need to question strongly whether the human person's true good can be defined as something that pertains to him or her as an individual alone, as much of modern thought wants to make us think. It would seem that human beings' true good must be thought of as some kind of life in community; they are not truly themselves as isolated individuals. This means that their true interest cannot be thought of apart from other people.[21] It is not in their interest to look out only for their own exclusive self-interest.

---

fullness of what he is by nature—that is, by himself—only in polis-like forms of living together" (my own translation).

19. Aristotle, *Politics*, I, 1, 1252b30–1253a1–5: "Nature is an end, since that which each thing is when its growth is completed we speak of as being the nature of each thing. . . . From these things therefore it is clear that the city-state is a natural growth [*tōn physei hē polis esti* = the city is of nature]."

20. Ibid., 1252b30.

21. See Melina, *Building a Culture*, 68–69: "[The idea of the common good] indicates that social relationships among human beings have an inherent goodness that should be safeguarded and promoted as essential to personal life. Against individualism—which thinks of persons as isolated monads and of relationships with others as something extrinsic and derived—we must recognize that it is only in lived relationships with the other and with others that an environment is created where each one can grow in his or her own humanity. The other person is not just a limit to my rights but a partner in a dialogue, who allows me to be fully aware of myself and to develop my personality."

But how can this *true* interest, which is not simply a private interest, be understood? To the modern mind it is difficult to imagine how to overcome the dialectic between egoism and altruism. Egoism is often thought of as the more or less natural human state, by which each pursues his or her own interests quite apart from those of everyone else, while altruism, by which one renounces one's interests for the sake of others, is as exceptional as it is mysterious and inexplicable in terms of human motivation, even though it appears desirable. Alasdair MacIntyre points out that "on the traditional Aristotelian view such problems do not arise." He continues, "What education in the virtues teaches me is that my good as a man is one and the same as the good of those others with whom I am bound up in human community. There is no way of my pursuing my good which is necessarily antagonistic to you pursuing yours because the good is neither mine peculiarly nor yours peculiarly—goods are not private property."[22] In other words, the way to overcome the dialectic between egoism and altruism lies in the notion of the *common good.*

Love and the Common Good

Love of the common good is a love that is neither egoistic—pursuing my good to the exclusion of the good of others—nor altruistic—pursuing the other's good to the exclusion of my own. It is loved not as my good or yours but as ours. In what follows we will examine more closely this connection between the common good and love. What understanding of the common good does one need to have to be able meaningfully to say that it is the object of love? As Pierpaolo Donati points out, the expression "common good" is often understood by economic theories as referring to *"the greatest possible good for the greatest possible number of individuals."* Such a definition of the common good "presents it as an entity that is convertible or reducible to the sum total of all the private interests of the individual members of a given society and interchangeable with them. In the prevailing definitions given by the social, economic and political sciences, the common good is *an allocation of resources such that everyone derives advantage from it."*[23] On this definition, "love" of the common good would have to be rather indirect. No one would, strictly speaking, seem to love a certain allocation of resources. At most one would "love" such allocation

22. MacIntyre, *After Virtue,* 229.
23. Donati, "Discovering the Relational Character," 660 (original emphases).

inasmuch as it is advantageous for that which one loves in the strict sense, which in turn is understood as private interest.

The traditional meaning of the common good is somewhat different and not at all antagonistic or indifferent to love. In fact, the common good is taken here as that which is most worthy of love, and not just merely as the condition of the possibility of the individual's private good; it is the individual's most authentic and proper and true good, loved not indirectly, but in the most authentic and proper sense. But what are the distinguishing features of the common good in the traditional sense, and how is it that it is loved even more properly than any private good? For the private good, Screwtape's observation mentioned above seems entirely valid: what is yours is not mine, what is mine is not yours. Though we do speak about *sharing* a meal with someone, the fact is that the particular portion of the dish that I eat another cannot eat. If I eat everything, the other is left with nothing. The money that is in my pocket is the money that is not in yours. I may indeed share these goods with others, but the more others partake in them, the less is left of them for me.

A common good is very different. The common good is a better, more noble good than a private good for reasons of its communicability: many can share in it without it thereby diminishing. The good is by nature diffusive. St. Thomas points out that the more diffusive and communicable a given good, the more excellent it is.[24] Besides, the common good is incommensurable and superabundant.[25] It cannot be exhausted by the individual, it cannot be completely seized by her or him; it is much larger than she or he is, so that it cannot be possessed as private property. St. Augustine gives us the example of the truth. Criticizing those who obstinately claim their own interpretation of Scripture to be the only legitimate one, not because it is true, but because it is theirs, he writes,

> They do not say this to me because they have a divine spirit and have seen in the heart of your servant what they assert, but because they are proud and have not known Moses's meaning, but love their own, not because it is true, but because it is their own.

24. See Aquinas, *Commentary on Aristotle's Nicomachean Ethics*, I, 2, 30: "Insofar as the good, which has the nature of a final cause, is more powerful, it extends to more effects."

25. See the very helpful discussion of the common good by De Koninck, "On the Primacy of the Common" and "In Defence of St. Thomas." De Koninck writes: "[A common good is] a good which because of its very superabundance is communicable to others" ("In Defence of St. Thomas," 269).

Otherwise, they would have an equal love for another man's true opinion, just as I love what they say when they speak the truth, not because it is theirs but because it is true. Therefore, because it is true it is by that very fact not theirs. Therefore, if they love it because it is true, then it is both theirs and mine, since it is the common property of all lovers of the truth. . . .

Whosoever arrogates completely to himself that which you propose for the enjoyment of all men, and desires that to be his own which belongs to all men, is driven from what is common to all men to what is really his own, that is from truth to a lie. For he who "speaks a lie speaks of his own."[26]

Truth is a common good. It is communicable to many. For example, my knowledge that two plus two equals four does not take away from anyone else's knowledge that things are this way. Moreover, is it not true that when a philosopher has a great insight or when a scientist makes a great discovery, usually the first thing he or she desires is to tell others about it? St. Augustine seems right: the truth that I keep for myself is nothing but a lie.

Another helpful example of a common good is a feast. Whose good is it? Does it belong to the host? There would not be any feast if the host were to remain by himself or herself. The feast is a good that can be had only in common with others. It is very significant that the image Scripture uses to describe heaven is precisely this: a feast, namely the wedding banquet of the Lamb,[27] thus showing us that the beatitude of the saints is a common good.

It is very significant and instructive that for St. Thomas, for example, God himself is loved by his creatures as a common good. He explains that the rational creature naturally loves God more than it loves itself for the reason that God is the common good of the whole universe and that the part naturally loves the whole more than that it loves itself as a part.[28] God is the common good of the universe, the final goal of all things, and has

26. Augustine, *Confessions*, Book XII, Chapter 25, 326.

27. See Revelation 19:7, 9: "Let us rejoice and exult and give him the glory, for the marriage of the Lamb has come, and his Bride has made herself ready. . . . Blessed are those who are invited to the marriage supper of the Lamb."

28. See Aquinas, *Summa Theologica*, I, 60, 5: "Since God is the universal good, and under this good both man and angel and all creatures are comprised, because every creature in regard to its entire being naturally belongs to God, it follows that from natural love angel and man alike love God before themselves and with a greater love. Otherwise, if either of them loved self more than God, it would follow that natural love would be perverse, and that it would not be perfected but destroyed by charity." See also ibid., II-II, 26, 3.

to be loved as such, i.e., God could never be loved by any creature as that creature's private good. Charles De Koninck comments on Aquinas's teaching with very helpful words: "If God had created and beatified but a single intellectual creature, He would still have to be loved in His communicability to other intellectual creatures. God is the *bonum universale simpliciter.* There can never be a proportion of equality between this infinite good and the intellectual creature's capacity for beatitude. The divine good can never be other than a common good for the creature."[29]

But there are still more earthly examples of common goods. Thus, the Angelic Doctor makes reference to the historian Valerius Maximus who says that the ancient Romans "preferred to be poor in a rich Empire than rich in a poor Empire."[30] This is possible of course only if they perceived the good of the Empire to be truly their own good. For them, there was no antagonism between their good and the good of the Empire simply because the good of the Empire was *their* good. From this it does not follow, however, that the individual could be sacrificed to the good of the whole. Here we may refer once more to Vladimir Solovyov, who emphasizes that the common good cannot be understood simply as the good of *many* or the good of the *majority*, but must be common in the fullest sense: it has to be "the good of *each.*" He continues:

> No one is excluded and, therefore, in serving *such* a social good as
> an end, the individual does *not* thereby become merely a means or
> an instrument of something extraneous and foreign to him. True
> society which recognizes the absolute right of each person is not
> the negative limit but the positive complement of the individual.
> In serving it with whole-hearted devotion, the individual does not
> lose but *realizes* his absolute worth and significance."[31]

If such is the nature of the common good—it is noble, superabundant, diffusive of itself, communicable to many, incommensurable to the individual, and yet the good of each—then it would seem to make a certain sense to say both: that it is something that is loved and that it is something at the basis of social life. Love and social life are profoundly connected in the notion of the common good: love of the common good is the corner stone of social life. It is the common good that unites people and keeps them from using each other as mere means to their private

---

29. De Koninck, "In Defence of St. Thomas," 263.
30. Aquinas, *Summa Theologica*, II-II, 47, 10, ad 2.
31. Solovyov, *Justification of the Good*, 230 (original emphases).

ends. It is the bond created by the common good that allows people to respect Kant's categorical imperative: "Act in such a way that you always treat humanity, whether in your own person or in the person of any other, never simply as a means, but always at the same time as an end."[32] Karol Wojtyła, explains this bond in this way:

> Obviously, I may want another person to desire the same good which I myself desire. Obviously, the other must know this end of mine, recognize it as a good, and adopt it. If this happens, a special bond is established between me and this other person: the bond of a *common good* and of a common aim. This special bond does not mean merely that we both seek a common good, it also unites the persons involved internally, and so constitutes the essential core round which any love must grow. In any case, love between two people is quite unthinkable without some common good to bind them together. This good is the end which both these persons choose. *When two different people consciously choose a common aim* this puts them on a footing of equality, and precludes the possibility that one of them might be subordinated to the other.[33]

However, we may wonder whether we do not use people all the time—whenever we go shopping for instance—or make use of other people's services to help us pursue our private ends. Is not my relationship to the merchant who sells me my food or to the taxi driver who gets me home one of merely using the other? Where would be the love of the common good in these cases? Alasdair MacIntyre grants to Adam Smith that it is not from the baker's charity that we hope to obtain our daily bread, but from the baker's own desire to make a living. Both of us seem to be pursuing simply our private interests, and yet even here a bond of civil friendship exists, though it may become clearly visible only in certain critical situations. MacIntyre writes, "if, on entering the butcher's shop as an habitual

---

32. Kant, *Groundwork*, 96.

33. Wojtyła, *Love and Responsibility*, 28–29 (original emphases). On this, see Buttiglione's comments on Wojtyła's notion of the common good in *Karol Wojtyła: The Thought of the Man*, 91: "How is it therefore possible to take the person as the object of one's act without undermining the personalistic norm? Only when two freedoms meet each other in the pursuit of a common good can the person be the object of reciprocal action conforming to the personalistic norm. . . . Love implies the freedom of the other and turns toward his good, through the discovery of an agreement or even an identity between *the other's good* and *one's own good*. In this way loving is the opposite of using" (original emphases). See also the very helpful discussion of Karol Wojtyła's notion of the common good found in Reimers, *Truth About the Good*.

customer I find him collapsing from a heart attack, and I merely remark 'Ah! Not in a position to sell me my meat to-day, I see,' and proceed immediately to his competitor's store to complete my purchase, I will have obviously and grossly damaged my *whole* relationship to him, including my economic relationship, although I will have done nothing contrary to the norms of the market."[34]

In other words, the economic relationship cannot be reduced to the principles of supply and demand that govern the market. At the very minimum the customer is related to the butcher by the bond of a civic friendship that is based on a good beyond their private interests and beyond the strict logic of the market. It is an original bond of which each is aware spontaneously and naturally. The ill butcher and his customer are related first of all and fundamentally by the fact of their common human personhood. Then, they are related by the fact of living and interacting in the same commonwealth and by civic virtues. In fact, as MacIntyre points out, "market relationships can only be sustained by being embedded in certain types of local nonmarket relationship, relationships of uncalculated giving and receiving."[35] This idea, of course, is echoed by Benedict XVI's encyclical *Caritas in Veritate*, where we read: "Authentically human social relationships of friendship, solidarity and reciprocity can also be conducted within economic activity, and not only outside it or 'after' it. The economic sphere is neither ethically neutral, nor inherently inhuman and opposed to society. It is part and parcel of human activity and precisely because it is human, it must be structured and governed in an ethical manner."[36]

Conclusion

What do we hope to have learned from these reflections about love and social life? We have said that human beings by nature are political animals, that their proper good is a common good and that therefore their proper love is of a common good. We have seen that there is no antagonism between an individual's true good and the common good, since the common good is precisely a person's true good. In this way the dialectic between egoism and altruism, of which MacIntyre speaks, can be overcome. Human beings are capable of benevolence in Leibniz' sense, i.e., they can take delight in

34. MacIntyre, *Dependent Rational Animals*, 117 (original emphasis).
35. Ibid.
36. Benedict XVI, *Caritas in Veritate*, no. 36.

the good of another.[37] Rejoicing in the good of another is possible because this good is, after all, not an alien good, precisely inasmuch as the other is not alien to be but invites me to communion. The antagonism between *my* good and *your* good is resolved in the recognition of *our* good, that is, in the dynamics of friendship.[38] From the perspective of friendship, human persons can understand even their own life and existence not only as their own good but also as the good of another. At one point, Robert Spaemann tells us how he has read a bumper sticker that said, "Think about your wife. Drive carefully."[39] This admonition presupposes a profound truth: human persons are capable of de-centering themselves, so to speak, of seeing themselves from the perspective of the other, and they can even love themselves from that perspective. For instance, a husband can love himself from the perspective of his wife, i.e., as her husband, as the one whom she loves and who is united to her by a special bond of friendship that implicates their whole lives. In other words, he is able to love even his own existence from the standpoint of the common good, inasmuch as his own life presents not simply his private good but constitutes an essential part of the common good that is his marriage, his family, his friendships.[40]

37. See Leibniz, *Codex Iuris Gentium*, 171: "Love . . . signifies rejoicing in the happiness of another."

38. See the very helpful description of marriage and the family as a common good, given by José Noriega, in his *Il destino dell'eros*, 71–72: "[It is] impossible to think of the fullness of the man or the woman or the children prescinding from the totality of the relationships in which they have found their place. The individual good of each of the spouses and the children and the good of the community, the marriage and the family are intrinsically related because the former can be seen and justified only in relation to the good of the community. That a man or a woman ask themselves about 'their proper good' means that they ask themselves about 'our good.' In this way pursuing my good means pursuing our good, the good of all those who participate in this relationship, the good of marriage, the good of the family" (my own translation).

39. Spaemann, *Happiness and Benevolence*, 94.

40. We may think here of Pope John Paul II's affirmation in his Letter to Families *Gratissimam Sane*, no. 11, where he calls the human person a "common good": "*A child comes to take up room, when it seems that there is less and less room in the world. But is it really true that a child brings nothing to the family and society? Is not every child a 'particle' of that common good without which human communities break down and risk extinction? . . . The common good of the whole of society dwells in man;* he is, as we recalled, 'the way of the Church.' Man is first of all the 'glory of God': '*Gloria Dei vivens homo,*' in the celebrated words of Saint Irenaeus, which might also be translated: 'the glory of God is for man to be alive.' It could be said that here we encounter the loftiest definition of man: *the glory of God is the common good of all that exists;* the common good of the human race. Yes! *Man is a common good*: a common good of the family and

144

The perfection of this attitude is assumed by the saints in heaven who, as Christians believe, take as much delight in another's beatitude as in their own because what they foremost love is the divine will. Thus, Piccarda, a blessed soul at the outskirts of heaven, when questioned whether she was happy where she was or whether she did not desire a higher place, responds to Dante in *The Divine Comedy*:

> Brother, love's virtue sets our will at rest,
>
> and makes us wish for only what we have,
>
> and doth not make us thirsty for aught else. . . .
>
> Essential to this blessed life it is,
>
> that we should be within the Will Divine,
>
> whereby our wills become one will;
>
> and so, even as we are, from grade to grade throughout this Realm,
>
> to all the Realm is pleasing, as to its King,
>
> who in His Will in-wills us;
>
> and His Will is our Peace.[41]

The philosophy of heaven, mysterious and apparently paradoxical though it is, is aptly described by Screwtape: "Now the Enemy's philosophy"—that is, from the perspective of a devil, God's own philosophy—"aims at a contradiction." We read on:

> Things are to be many, yet somehow also one. The good of one self is to be the good of another. This impossibility He calls *love*, and this same monotonous panacea can be detected under all He does and even all He is—or claims to be. Thus He is not content, even Himself, to be a sheer arithmetical unity; He claims to be three as well as one, in order that this nonsense about Love may find a foothold in His own nature.[42]

If this is the way things are, if the good of one self is also the good of another, if love, understood as the communication in the good by which persons are bound together, is the fundamental reality, then the words of Alasdair MacIntyre are profoundly true: "The egoist is . . . always someone who

---

of humanity, of individual groups and of different communities" (original emphases). See the very enlightening comments of Michael Waldstein on this passage in "The Common Good," 575–77.

41. Dante, *Divine Comedy III, Paradiso*, III, 70–72, 79–85.

42. Lewis, *Screwtape Letters*, 94 (original emphasis).

has made a fundamental mistake about where his own good lies."[43] Kant's devils will then not be quite as intelligent as he makes them out to be, and love—i.e., love of the common good—will be the cornerstone of social life.

43. MacIntyre, *After Virtue*, 229.

9

Ab Urbe Condita:
Arendt and Authority

But the centurion answered him, "Lord, I am not worthy to have you come under my roof; but only say the word, and my servant will be healed. For I am a man under authority, with soldiers under me; and I say to one, 'Go,' and he goes, and to another, 'Come,' and he comes, and to my slave, 'Do this,' and he does it." When Jesus heard him, he marveled, and said to those who followed him, "Truly, I say to you, not even in Israel have I found such faith."

—MATT 8:8–10

The Loss of Authority

ALREADY MORE THAN HALF a century ago, Hannah Arendt spoke of a "breakdown of authority" which can be witnessed in our Western world.[1] We can only speculate what she would call today's situation, which has certainly not become any better. There are increasing reports of violence in schools, and teachers often have to spend more time on disciplining their pupils than on teaching them. Frequently, the relationship between parents and their own children is not much better, and many times parents relinquish

1. Arendt, "Breakdown of Authority."

147

their educational rights and obligations to television or to video games.

The loss of authority is not restricted to the realm of education, but permeates society as a whole, including the realm of government. Few citizens of our Western democracies would call the political leaders they voted into office by the name of "authority." Usually, a president, prime minister, or chancellor is not considered an authority but rather an administrator, who fulfills his or her job sometimes for good, sometimes for ill. At one point, police officers in England had so much authority that they did not need to carry firearms, but these times, too, have long since drawn to an end.[2]

In this chapter I would like to offer some reflections on the roots of today's loss of authority, basing myself on Hannah Arendt's thought on this topic. I shall first begin with a phenomenal description of authority and thereby also distinguish it from what it is not. Next I will discuss the sources of authentic authority and finally attempt to show how the breakdown of authority is related to what Arendt calls the modern-day phenomenon of "world alienation."[3]

Authority and Its Counterfeits

Authority has something to do with commanding and obeying. Persons who have authority tell persons under their authority to do something and the latter do so. We can think here of the parent-child relationship, the teacher-student relationship, perhaps the officer-soldier relationship, and in general the relationship between persons whose words have weight and the people who care to listen. If parents or teachers have authority, the children or students obey at their mere word. It is the same with all other persons in authority and those they are commanding.

However, Hannah Arendt warns us that "since authority always demands obedience, it is commonly mistaken for some form of power or violence."[4] In fact, there are people who command and expect obedience because they have superior force and threaten violence in case of disobedience. Yet, authority is not the same as force or violence. Rather, it is evident that a parent or a teacher who constantly has to threaten sanctions to obtain a coerced obedience has already lost all authority. Arendt is quite to the point

2. See for instance Ingleton, *Arming the British Police.*

3. See Arendt, *Human Condition,* 248–57.

4. Arendt, "What Is Authority?" 92.

when she explains that one-party regimes that are called "authoritarian" are actually quite the contrary of authoritarian.[5] When violence in any form needs to be threatened to make people obey, this is a sign that authority has been lost. Arendt writes, "Authority precludes the use of external means of coercion; where force is used, authority itself has failed."[6]

Mistaking authority for force or violence is a common mistake. When Pope Pius VII drafted a bull of excommunication against Napoleon, the French leader derided him and scornfully wrote to Eugene Beauharnais: "Does he fancy his excommunication will make the sabers fall from the hands of my grenadiers?"[7] Incidentally, this is exactly what happened during Napoleon's ill-fated Russian campaign, however we shall presume for reasons other than the pope's intervention. On Pope Pius XI's condemnation of communism, Stalin, too, famously voiced his incomprehension, asking "How many divisions does the pope have?"[8] Both dictators mistook authority for violence or force, being unable to see how the words of those who do not have armies at their command could have any weight.

Authority is not the same as expertise either. Experts, too, "command" and people obey, but the reason they obey is not the experts' authority but their presumed knowledge. Ultimately, experts persuade by means of arguments, and, as Arendt points out, the use of arguments always presupposes a fundamental equality, which is contrary to the notion of authority, however one wants to define it:

> Authority . . . is incompatible with persuasion, which presupposes equality and works through a process of argumentation. Where arguments are used, authority is left in abeyance. Against the egalitarian order of persuasion stands the authoritarian order, which is always hierarchical. If authority is to be defined at all, then, it must be in contradistinction to both coercion by force and persuasion through arguments.[9]

In the case of experts, it is their knowledge that commands; the experts can step back, as it were, and let the facts speak for themselves. The

---

5. See Arendt, "Breakdown of Authority": "One-party regimes call themselves 'authoritarian.' They come after authority has broken down, but are the contrary of 'authoritarian.'"

6. Arendt, "What Is Authority?" 92.

7. Olf, *Their Name Is Pius,* 102.

8. See Dunn, *Catholic Church and Russia,* 91.

9. Arendt, "What Is Authority?" 92–93.

experts are the mere mouthpiece of the simple facts. Thus, they are not personally involved in the advice they gives; people do not obey them as persons who have a specific place in a hierarchy, but they simply believe their word that the facts are of a certain kind. Charles de Gaulle is reported to have said, "There are three roads to ruin: by gambling, which is the quickest; through women, which is the most pleasurable; and through taking the advice of experts, which is the most certain." Given our above reflections, this somewhat cynical remark may have a basis in fact: In giving their advice, the experts can hide behind their knowledge. They do not have to assume personal responsibility for their advice; they can simply refer to "the way things are." This is why their advice can in fact become literally irresponsible.

The Source of Authority: The Foundation of the "Public Thing"

Even though authority is not the same as violence or expertise, it is nonetheless a reality and a marvelous one at that. When we lend an ear to the great men and women of our times, whether they are religious leaders or statesmen, when the words of Pope John Paul II were respected by believers and unbelievers alike, when children obey their father without need for explanation or threat—i.e., not on the grounds of their father's superior expertise or force but simply because he is their father—when students obey their teachers because they are their teachers and not because of possible sanctions but simply on their word, then we witness instances of authority that are still left, even in our own day and age. And the question is: What is the basis of this mysterious power, if it is neither founded on force or violence, nor on expertise?

According to Hannah Arendt, the notion of authority goes back to classical Roman times and was intimately connected to the foundation of the City. "The foundation of a new body politic . . . became to the Romans the central, decisive, unrepeatable beginning of their whole history, a unique event."[10] This is the event that provides the context for understanding the concept of authority:

> The word *auctoritas* derives from the verb *augere*, "augment," and what authority or those in authority constantly augment is the

10. Ibid., 120.

foundation. Those endowed with authority were the elders, the Senate or the *patres*, who had obtained it by descent and by transmission (tradition) from those who had laid the foundations for all things to come, the ancestors, whom the Romans therefore called the *maiores*. The authority of the living was always derivative, depending upon the *auctores imperii Romani conditoresque . . .* upon the authority of the founders, who no longer were among the living. Authority, in contradistinction to power . . . had its roots in the past, put this past was no less present in the actual life of the city than the power and strength of the living.[11]

Insofar as it is tied up to an event of the past, i.e., the foundation that serves as the point of reference for any decision, authority has what one can call a "transcendent" source. It goes beyond the individual who has it and is recognized by both those in command and those obeying. In her unpublished paper "Breakdown of Authority," Arendt expresses this idea most succinctly:

> Authority, though it expresses itself in a relationship between one who commands and others who obey, does not rest on violence and arbitrariness. Authority presupposes that both those who command and those who obey have in common to recognize the legitimacy of the command. Authority and legitimacy: Those who command have a right to command and their commands are based on something recognized by both.[12]

The one who commands with authority and the one who obeys are both united by a bond of common belief and common concern. Both those who command and those who obey need to live in and be concerned about a common world. For the ancient Romans, this common world was the City, the Empire, the *res publica*, which was constituted by an event: the foundation of the City. This foundational event was handed on to each new generation and remained the reference point for all authority.

For Arendt, after the decline of the Roman Empire, it was the Catholic Church that in some way inherited the Roman legacy and that still today represents authentic authority.[13] To her mind, authority is always part of a "trinity" made up of religion, which re-binds us to the past (religion deriv-

11. Ibid., 121–22.

12. Arendt, "Breakdown of Authority."

13. For Arendt's claim that authority has lost its role in politics today and more or less continues to be represented only in the Catholic Church, see the German version of her essay "What Is Authority?": Arendt, "Was ist Autorität?" 169.

ing etymologically from *re-ligare*, i.e., "re-binding"[14]); authority, which is the notion under discussion here; and tradition, which is the way the past is handed on: "Thanks to the fact that the foundation of the city of Rome was repeated in the foundation of the Catholic Church, though, of course, with a radically different content, the Roman trinity of religion, authority, and tradition could be taken over by the Christian era."[15]

For Christians, the foundation of the church, analogously to the foundation of the City of Rome, was likewise constituted by an event: the death and resurrection of Jesus Christ. This foundational event, too, is being handed on from generation to generation, and those in authority in the church are vested with authority precisely insofar as they are witnessing to that event:

> The Church . . . made the death and resurrection of Christ the cornerstone of a new foundation, erecting on it a new human institution of tremendous durability. . . . As witnesses to this event the Apostles could become the "founding fathers" of the Church, from whom she would derive her own authority as long as she handed down their testimony by way of tradition from generation to generation.[16]

In the case of both the Roman Empire and the Catholic Church, authority is based on something that is at the same time greater than the individual and common to those who are in authority and those who are under it. Authority is based on a public thing, a *res publica*, a common good and a common concern, whether it is the foundation of the city or the foundation of the church. What for Arendt distinguishes those in authority is that they are *willing to take responsibility* for this common world or this common good. According to her, "wherever true authority existed it was joined with responsibility for the course of things in the world."[17]

Thus, in education, for instance, the willingness to take responsibility for the world expresses itself in a person's readiness to introduce newcomers into it.[18] Unless people are interested in the common world, all they will

---

14. See Arendt, "What Is Authority?" 121, "Here religion literally meant *re-ligare*: to be tied back, obligated to the enormous, almost superhuman and hence always legendary effort to lay the foundations, to build the cornerstone, to found for eternity."

15. Ibid., 126.

16. Ibid., 125–26.

17. Arendt, "Crisis in Education," 186 (emphasis added).

18. See Mordechai, "Hannah Arendt on Authority," 46: "To demand of parents and

have to say to the new generation is, in Arendt's words: "In this world even we are not very securely at home; how to move about in it, what to know, what skills to master, are mysteries to us too. You must try to make out as best you can; in any case you are not entitled to call us to account. We are innocent, we wash our hands of you."[19]

To have authority one needs to live one's life under the horizon of something that is greater than one's own life and one needs to be willing to take responsibility for it. In a sense, the person in authority him- or herself always stands under authority, namely under the authority of the foundational event that constituted the common world, whether it is the foundation of the city, the laying down of the constitution, or—in the case of the church—the death and resurrection of Christ. *Only someone under authority can have authority.*

When Life Becomes the Highest Good: Authority and the Problem of "World Alienation"

Now, in a final step, we will turn to the possible roots of today's widespread breakdown of authority and propose one aspect of it that we can draw from Hannah Arendt's insightful analysis in *The Human Condition*. In this central work, Arendt traces the way human activities have been valued and evaluated from classical Greek and Roman times to modernity. The conclusion of her study is that what she calls the *animal laborans,* the human person as laboring being, concerned with making a living, has won the day both over *homo faber*—the human person as a working being, concerned with the construction of an external world—and over the acting and interacting person, concerned with relating to others and building a web of interpersonal relationships.[20] Arendt points out that for today's public opinion the entire vast variety of possible human activities can be put into just two categories: laboring and playing.[21] To labor is the only serious activity, and it

---

teachers that they assume responsibility for the world into which they introduce the young, as she [Arendt] does, presupposes that responsibility and freedom are fundamental possibilities of the human condition. In fact, she believes that the current loss of authority in education was partly brought about by parents and teachers who refused to assume this responsibility."

19. Arendt, "Crisis in Education," 188.

20. See Arendt, *Human Condition,* 320–25. This final section is entitled "The Victory of the *Animal Laborans."*

21. See ibid., 126–27: "Whatever we do, we are supposed to do for the sake of 'making

is tantamount to making a living. When one is not laboring one is playing. In a society of job-holders, even the work of a prime minister is considered a way of making a living. The same holds true for doctors, lawyers, actors, and pastors of souls.

It is clear that in a society where the highest activity of which the human person is capable is providing for his or her own life and survival, the person's individual life will be regarded as the highest good.[22] In this context, Hannah Arendt speaks of "world-alienation." People are being alienated from the world, from what is public and common and are thrown back upon themselves.[23] The life of the individual becomes the highest good, so that people's interest in the common thing, the *res publica* comes to naught. Yet, where there is no interest in the public thing, there can be no authority, as authority presupposes the reference to something that is common to all and that is higher than the life of each, namely the common world, whatever form it may take.

Ultimately, only persons who are willing to lay down their life for something greater than their own life can have authority. In a society where life is the highest good, there can be no authority, because there is no authentic concern for a true common good. The gospel words hold true, both for individuals and for societies: "Whoever would save his life will lose it; and whoever loses his life for my sake, he will save it" (Luke 9:24). For Christians, the church is the new *res publica*, but this does not deny the existence of a true common good on earth, nor does the church stand in contrast to the earthly common good. In fact, in a very intriguing passage Hannah Arendt relates the modern-day crisis of the faith to the loss of a sense for the common world.[24] People have lost the very idea of something greater than the care of their own private lives, whether it is the common

---

a living'; such is the verdict of society, and the number of people, especially in the professions, who might challenge it, has decreased rapidly.... The same trend to level down all serious activities to the status of making a living is manifest in present-day labor theories, which almost unanimously define labor as the opposite of play."

22. See ibid., 313–20.

23. See ibid., 254.

24. See Arendt, *Human Condition*, 253–54: "Modern loss of faith is not religious in origin . . . and its scope is by no means restricted to the religious sphere. Moreover, even if we admitted that the modern age began with a sudden, inexplicable eclipse of transcendence . . . it would by no means follow that this loss threw man back upon the world. The historical evidence, on the contrary, shows that modern men were not thrown back upon this world but upon themselves. . . . World alienation, and not self-alienation as Marx thought, has been the hallmark of the modern age."

world or the kingdom of heaven, which already breaks into the world today. Yet, if we have nothing to die for, we will have nothing to live for. Thus, if we look at the great people of our own age who certainly had authority, like St. John Paul II, for instance, we see that they had something to live and something to die for and that it is precisely here that we find the source of their authority. To stay with the example, John Paul II clearly lived all his life in reference to something greater, something that was entrusted to him, that he did not think he owned, and that he passed on faithfully, something · that others, too, could recognize, acknowledge and share in. In this sense, he, too, like the centurion that met Jesus in the biblical episode, was a man of authority because he was a man under authority.

Bibliography

Acosta, Miguel, and Adrian J. Reimers. *Karol Wojtyła's Personalist Philosophy: Understanding Person & Act*. Washington, DC: Catholic University of America Press, 2016.

Anderson, Carl A., and José Granados. *Called to Love: Approaching John Paul II's Theology of the Body*. New York: Doubleday, 2009.

Aquinas, Thomas. *Commentary on Aristotle's Nicomachean Ethics*. Translated by C. I. Litzinger. Notre Dame: Dumb Ox, 1993.

————. *Commentary on the Letter of Paul to the Romans*, Latin-English Edition. Translated by R. F. Larcher. Lander, WY: Aquinas Institute for the Study of Sacred Doctrine, 2012.

————. *Commentary on St. Matthew's Gospel*. Translated by R. F. Larcher. http://www.dhspriory.org/thomas/SSMatthew.htm.

————. *Summa Contra Gentiles*. Translated by Anthony C. Pegis. New York: Hanover House, 1955.

————. *Summa Theologica*. Translated by Fathers of the English Dominican Province. New York: Benzinger Brothers, 1947–48.

————. *Truth*. Translated by R. W. Mulligan. Indianapolis: Hackett, 1954.

Archer, Margaret S., and Pierpaolo Donati, eds. *Pursuing the Common Good: How Solidarity and Subsidiarity Can Work Together*. Vatican City: Pontifical Academy of Social Sciences, 2008.

Arendt, Hannah. "Breakdown of Authority." Unnumbered typescript of a lecture held at New York University, New York, dated November 23, 1953. Hannah Arendt Papers, Manuscript Division, Library of Congress, Washington, DC. http://memory.loc.gov/cgi-bin/ampage?collId=mharendt&fileName=05/05108a/05108apage.db&recNum=0.

————. "Concluding Remarks." In *The Origins of Totalitarianism*, 429–39. New York: Harcourt Brace, 1951.

————. "Crisis in Education." In *Between Past and Future: Eight Exercises in Political Thought*, 170–93. New York: Penguin, 2006.

―――. "The Eggs Speak Up." In *Essays in Understanding, 1930–1954*, edited by Jerome Kohn, 270–84. New York: Harcourt, 1994.

―――. *Eichmann in Jerusalem: A Report on the Banality of Evil.* New York: Penguin, 1994.

―――. *The Human Condition.* 2nd ed. Chicago: University of Chicago Press, 1998.

―――. *The Life of the Mind.* One-volume ed. Edited by Mary McCarthy. New York: Harcourt, Brace, 1978.

―――. *Love and Saint Augustine.* Edited by Joanna Vecchiarelli Scott and Judith Chelius Stark. Chicago: University of Chicago Press, 1996.

―――. "On Hannah Arendt." In *Hannah Arendt: The Recovery of the Public World*, edited by Melvyn A. Hill, 301–39. New York: St. Martin's, 1979.

―――. *The Origins of Totalitarianism.* New ed. New York: Harcourt, 1968.

―――. "Some Questions of Moral Philosophy." In *Responsibility and Judgment*, edited by Jerome Kohn, 49–146. New York: Schocken, 2003.

―――. "Was ist Autorität?" In *Zwischen Vergangenheit und Zukunft: Übungen im politischen Denken I*, 159–200. Munich: Piper, 1994.

―――. "What Is Authority?" In *Between Past and Future: Eight Exercises in Political Thought*, 91–141. New York: Penguin, 2006.

―――. "What Is Existential Philosophy?" In *Essays in Understanding, 1930–1954*, edited by Jerome Kohn, 163–87. New York: Harcourt, 1994.

Arendt, Hannah, and Mary McCarthy. *Between Friends: The Correspondence of Hannah Arendt and Mary McCarthy, 1949–1975.* Edited by Carol Brightman. New York: Harcourt Brace, 1995.

Aristotle. *Metaphysics.* Translated by W. D. Ross. Oxford: Clarendon 1924.

―――. *The Nicomachean Ethics.* Translated by H. Rackham. Cambridge, MA: Harvard University Press, 1934.

―――. *On the Soul.* Translated by J. A. Smith. Oxford: Clarendon, 1931.

―――. *Physics.* Translated by R. P. Hardie and R. K. Gaye. Oxford: Clarendon, 1930.

―――. *Politics.* Translated by H. Rackham. Cambridge, MA: Harvard University Press, 1944.

―――. *Topica.* Translated by E. S. Forster. Cambridge, MA: Harvard University Press, 1960.

Augustine. *The City of God.* Translated by Henry Bettenson. New York: Penguin, 1984.

―――. *The Confessions of St. Augustine.* Translated by John K. Ryan. New York: Image, 1960.

―――. *On Free Choice of the Will.* Translated by Anna S. Benjamin and L. H. Hackstaff. New York: Macmillan, 1964.

―――. *On the Trinity: Books 8–15.* Edited by Gareth Matthews. Translated by Stephen McKenna. Cambridge: Cambridge University Press, 2002.

―――. *Our Lord's Sermon on the Mount.* In vol. 6 of *Nicene and Post-Nicene Fathers*, series I. Edited by Philip Schaff. Edinburgh: T. & T. Clark, 1887.

―――. *Sermons on Selected Lessons of the New Testament.* In vol. 6 of *Nicene and Post-Nicene Fathers*, series I. Edited by Philip Schaff. Edinburgh: T. & T. Clark, 1887.

Barth, Karl. *Church Dogmatics, I/1: The Doctrine of the Word of God.* Translated by G. W. Bromiley and T. F. Torrance. London: T. & T. Clark, 2004.

Bassett, William, and Peter Huizing, eds. *Judgment in the Church.* New York: Seabury, 1977.

Belardinelli, Sergio. *Bioetica tra natura e cultura.* Siena: Cantagalli, 2007.

Benedict XVI, Pope. "Address to Participants in the Meeting Promoted by the Pontifical John Paul II Institute for Studies on Marriage and Family." May 13, 2011.

———. *Caritas in Veritate*. Encyclical Letter, June 29, 2009.

———. *Deus Caritas Est*. Encyclical Letter, December 25, 2005.

———. "Meeting with the Authorities and the Diplomatic Corps." Hofburg, Vienna, September 7, 2007.

———. *Spe Salvi*. Encyclical Letter, November 30, 2007.

Berkman, John, and William C. Mattison III, eds. *Searching for a Universal Ethic: Multidisciplinary, Ecumenical and Interfaith Responses to the Catholic Natural Law Tradition*. Grand Rapids: Eerdmans, 2014.

Blondel, Maurice. *Action (1893): Essay on a Critique of Life and a Science of Practice*. Translated by Oliva Blanchette. Notre Dame: University of Notre Dame Press, 2003.

Bonhoeffer, Dietrich. *Act and Being: Transcendental Philosophy and Ontology in Systematic Theology*. Edited by Wayne Whitson Floyd Jr. Translated by H. M. Rumscheidt. Minneapolis: Fortress, 1996.

Bonstein, Julia, et al. "Wer melkt wen?" *Der Spiegel*, August 6, 2007, 18–21.

Botturi, Francesco. *La generazione del bene: Gratuità ed esperienza morale*. Milan: Vita e Pensiero, 2009.

Brecht, Bertolt. "The Buddha's Parable of the Burning House." In *Poems, 1913–1956*, edited by John Willett and Ralph Manheim with the cooperation of Erich Fried, 290–92. New York: Routledge, 1987.

Buttiglione, Rocco. *Karol Wojtyła: The Thought of the Man Who Became Pope John Paul II*. Translated by Paolo Guietti and Francesca Murphy. Grand Rapids: Eerdmans, 1997.

Camus, Albert. *The Myth of Sisyphus, and Other Essays*. Translated by Justin O'Brien. New York: Vintage, 1991.

Chesterton, Gilbert Keith. *Orthodoxy*. San Francisco: Ignatius, 1995.

Chrysostom, John. *Homilies on Matthew*. In vol. 10 of *Nicene and Post-Nicene Fathers*, series I. Edited by Philip Schaff. Edinburgh: T. & T. Clark, 1888.

Cicero, Marcus Tullius. *Tusculan Disputations*. In *Academic Questions, Treatise De Finibus, and Tusculan Disputations*, translated by C. D. Yonge, 284–474. London: Bohn, 1853.

Clarke, William Norris. "Person, Being, and St. Thomas." *Communio* 19 (1992) 601–18.

Curran, Charles E., and Richard A. McCormick, eds. *Dissent in the Church*. Mahwah, NJ: Paulist, 1988.

Dante Alighieri. *The Divine Comedy*. Translated by Courtney Langdon. 3 vols. Cambridge, MA: Harvard University Press, 1918–21.

Dawkins, Richard. *The God Delusion*. London: Transworld, 2006.

———. *The Selfish Gene*. Oxford: Oxford University Press, 2006.

De Koninck, Charles. "In Defence of St. Thomas." In vol. 2 of *The Writings of Charles De Koninck*, edited and translated by Ralph McInerny, 205–63. Notre Dame: University of Notre Press, 2009.

———. "On the Primacy of the Common Good: Against the Personalists." In vol. 2 of *The Writings of Charles De Koninck*, edited and translated by Ralph McInerny, 65–108. Notre Dame: University of Notre Press, 2009.

Derrida, Jacques. *Given Time: I. Counterfeit Money*. Translated by Peggy Kamuf. Chicago: University of Chicago Press, 1992.

Donati, Pierpaolo. "Discovering the Relational Character of the Common Good." In *Pursuing the Common Good: How Solidarity and Subsidiarity Can Work Together*, edited by Margaret Archer and Pierpaolo Donati, 659–83. Vatican City: Pontifical Academy of Social Sciences, 2008.

Dostoevsky, Fyodor. *The Brothers Karamazov*. Translated by Constance Garnett. New York: Lowell, 1912.

Dunn, Dennis J. *The Catholic Church and Russia: Popes, Patriarchs, Tsars, and Commissars*. Aldershot, UK: Ashgate, 2004.

Eliot, T. S. "Choruses from 'The Rock.'" In *The Complete Poems and Plays*, 147–67. London: Faber and Faber, 2004.

Epictetūs. *Enchiridion*. Translated by George Long. Mineola, NY: Dover Thrift, 2004.

The Epistle to Diognetus. In *Early Christian Writings: The Apostolic Fathers*, translated by Maxwell Staniforth, 142–51. Revised translations by Andrew Louth. New York: Penguin Classics, 1987.

Erikson, Erik Homburger. "The Problem of Ego Identity." *Journal of the American Psychoanalytic Association* 4 (1956) 56–121.

Flores d'Arcais, Paolo. *"La democrazia ha bisogno di Dio"—Falso!* Roma-Bari: Laterza, 2013.

Francis, Pope. "Address to Members of the International Theological Commission." December 6, 2013.

———. "Address to Participants in the Commemorative Conference of the Italian Catholic Physicians' Association on the Occasion of Its 70th Anniversary of Foundation." November 15, 2014.

———. "Concluding Address of the Fourteenth Ordinary General Assembly of the Synod of Bishops." October 24, 2015.

———. *Evangelii Gaudium*. Apostolic Exhortation, November 24, 2013.

———. *Lumen Fidei*. Encyclical Letter, June 29, 2013.

Frankfurt, Harry G. *The Importance of What We Care About: Philosophical Essays*. Cambridge: Cambridge University Press, 1998.

Giddens, Anthony. *The Transformation of Intimacy: Sexuality, Love and Eroticism in Modern Societies*. Cambridge: Polity, 1993.

Godbout, Jacques T., and Alain Caillé. *The World of the Gift*. Translated by Donald Winkler. Montreal: McGill-Queen's University Press, 1998.

Goodchild, Peter. *Robert Oppenheimer: Shatterer of Worlds*. Mount Prospect, IL: Fromm International, 1985.

Granados, José. "Love and the Organism: A Theological Contribution to the Study of Life." *Communio* 32 (2005) 19–51.

Gregory, Brad S. *The Unintended Reformation: How a Religious Revolution Secularized Society*. Cambridge, MA: Belknap Press of Harvard University Press, 2012.

Grygiel, Stanisław. *Extra comunionem personarum nulla philosophia*. Rome: Lateran University Press, 2002.

Guardini, Romano. *The World and the Person*. Translated by Stella Lange. Chicago: H. Regnery, 1965.

Habermas, Jürgen. *The Future of Human Nature*. Cambridge: Polity, 2003.

———. "Kant's Idea of Perpetual Peace: At Two Hundred Years' Historical Remove." In *The Inclusion of the Other: Studies in Political Theory*, edited by Ciaran Cronin and Pablo De Greiff, 165–202. Cambridge, UK: Polity, 1999.

Hahn, Scott. *Kinship by Covenant: A Canonical Approach to the Fulfillment of God's Saving Promises*. New Haven: Yale University Press, 2009.

Heidegger, Martin. *Being and Time*. Translated by Joan Stambaugh. Albany: State University of New York Press, 1996.

———. "The Onto-theo-logical Constitution of Metaphysics." In *Identity and Difference*, translated by Joan Stambaugh, 42–74. Chicago: University of Chicago Press, 2002.

———. *Pathmarks*. Edited by William McNeill. Cambridge: Cambridge University Press, 1998.

Hill, John Lawrence. *After the Natural Law: How the Classical Worldview Supports Our Modern Moral and Political Values*. San Francisco: Ignatius, 2016.

Hill, Melvyn A., ed. *Hannah Arendt: The Recovery of the Public World*. New York: St. Martin's, 1979.

Hiltunen, Ari. *Aristotle in Hollywood: The Anatomy of Successful Storytelling*. Bristol: Intellect, 2002.

Hobbes, Thomas. *Leviathan*. Edited by John Charles Addison Gaskin. Oxford: Oxford University Press, 2008.

———. *Man and Citizen: De Homine and De Cive*. Edited by Bernard Gert. Indianapolis: Hackett, 1998.

Hume, David. *A Treatise of Human Nature: A Critical Edition*. Edited by David Fate Norton and Mary J. Norton. Oxford: Clarendon, 2007.

Huxley, Aldous. *Brave New World*. London: Chatto & Windus, 1932.

Ingleton, Roy D. *Arming the British Police: The Great Debate*. London: Frank Cass, 1996.

International Theological Commission. *In Search of a Universal Ethic: A New Look at the Natural Law*. 2009. http://www.vatican.va/roman_curia/congregations/cfaith/cti_documents/rc_con_cfaith_doc_20090520_legge-naturale_en.html.

———. *Sensus Fidei in the Life of the Church*. 2014. http://www.vatican.va/roman_curia/congregations/cfaith/cti_documents/rc_cti_20140610_sensus-fidei_en.html.

John Paul II, Pope. "Address to UNESCO." June 2, 1980.

———. *Ecclesia de Eucharistia*. Encyclical Letter, April 17, 2003.

———. *Gratissimam Sane*. Letter to Families, February 2, 1994.

———. *Redemptoris Mater*. Encyclical Letter, March 25, 1987.

———. *Veritatis Splendor*. Encyclical Letter, August 6, 1993.

Jonas, Hans. "Contemporary Problems in Ethics from a Jewish Perspective." In *Philosophical Essays: From Ancient Creed to Technological Man*, 168–82. Chicago: University of Chicago Press, 1974.

———. *The Imperative of Responsibility: In Search of an Ethics for the Technological Age*. Chicago: University of Chicago Press, 1984.

———. *The Phenomenon of Life: Toward a Philosophical Biology*. Evanston: Northwestern University Press, 2001.

———. "Philosophy at the End of the Century: A Survey of Its Past and Future." *Social Research* 61 (1994) 812–32.

———. "Toward a Philosophy of Technology." *Hastings Center Report* 9 (1979) 34–43.

Kampowski, Stephan. *Arendt, Augustine, and the New Beginning: The Action Theory and Moral Thought of Hannah Arendt in the Light of Her Dissertation on St. Augustine*. Grand Rapids: Eerdmans, 2008.

———. *A Greater Freedom: Biotechnology, Love and Human Destiny (In Dialogue with Hans Jonas and Jürgen Habermas)*. Eugene, OR: Pickwick, 2013.

Kant, Immanuel. *Critique of Judgement*. Translated by James Creed Meredith. Revised, edited, and introduced by Nicholas Walker. Oxford: Oxford University Press, 2007.

————. *Groundwork of the Metaphysics of Morals.* Translated by H. J. Paton. New York: Harper, 1964.

————. *To Perpetual Peace: A Philosophical Sketch.* Translated by Ted Humphrey. Indianapolis: Hackett, 2003.

Kasper, Walter. *The Gospel of the Family.* Translated by William Madges. Mahwah, NJ: Paulist, 2014.

Kass, Leon. *Life, Liberty and the Defense of Dignity: The Challenge for Bioethics.* San Francisco: Encounter, 2002.

————. "Looking Good: Nature and Nobility." In *Toward a More Natural Science: Biology and Human Affairs,* 318–45. New York: Free, 1985.

Kierkegaard, Søren. *Papers and Journals: A Selection.* Translated by Alastair Hannay. New York: Penguin Classics, 1996.

Krausz, Michael, ed. *Relativism: Interpretation and Confrontation.* Notre Dame: University of Notre Dame Press, 1989.

Küng, Hans. *Global Responsibility: In Search of a New World Ethic.* Translated by John Bowden. New York: Crossroad, 1991.

Kupczak, Jarosław. *Gift and Communion: John Paul II's Theology of the Body.* Washington, DC: Catholic University of America Press, 2014.

Larrú, Juan de Dios. "The Original Source of Love: The Pierced Heart." In *The Way of Love: Reflections on Pope Benedict XVI's Encyclical Deus Caritas Est,* edited by Livio Melina and Carl A. Anderson, 199–211. San Francisco: Ignatius, 2006.

Leibniz, Gottfried Wilhelm. *Codex Iuris Gentium (Praefatio)* (1693). In *Political Writings,* edited by Patrick Riley, 165–76. Cambridge: Cambridge University Press, 1988.

Leo XIII, Pope. *Libertas Praestantissimum.* Encyclical Letter, June 20, 1888.

Levada, William. "Dissent and the Catholic Religion Teacher." In *Dissent in the Church,* edited by Charles E. Curran and Richard A. McCormick, 133–51. Mahwah, NJ: Paulist, 1988.

Levinas, Emmanuel. *Ethics and Infinity: Conversations with Philippe Nemo.* Translated by Richard A. Cohen. Pittsburgh: Duquesne University Press, 1985.

————. *Totality and Infinity: An Essay on Exteriority.* Translated by Alphonso Lingis. Pittsburgh: Duquesne University Press, 1969.

Lévi-Strauss, Claude. "The Family." In *Man, Culture and Society,* edited by Harry L. Shapiro, 333–57. Oxford: Oxford University Press, 1971.

————. *Race and History.* Paris: UNESCO, 1952.

Lewis, Clive Staples. *The Abolition of Man: How Education Develops Man's Sense of Morality.* New York: Macmillan, 1947.

————. *The Four Loves.* New York: Harcourt Brace, 1960.

————. *The Screwtape Letters.* New York: HarperCollins, 2001.

López, Antonio. *Gift and the Unity of Being.* Eugene, OR: Cascade, 2014.

MacIntyre, Alasdair. *After Virtue: A Study in Moral Theory.* 2nd ed. Notre Dame: University of Notre Dame Press, 1984.

————. *Dependent Rational Animals: Why Human Beings Need the Virtues.* Chicago: Open Court, 1999.

Mansini, Guy. *Promising and the Good.* Naples, FL: Sapientia Press of Ave Maria University, 2005.

Marcel, Gabriel. *Being and Having.* Translated by Katharine Farrer. Westminster: Dacre, 1949.

Marion, Jean-Luc. *Being Given: Toward a Phenomenology of Givenness*. Translated by Jeffrey L. Kosky. Stanford: Stanford University Press, 2002.

———. *God Without Being*. Translated by Thomas A. Carlson. Chicago: University of Chicago Press, 1991.

Marx, Karl. *Capital: A Critique of Political Economy*. Vol. 1. Translated by Ben Fowkes. New York: Vintage, 1977.

———. *Critique of the Gotha Programme*. In *Selected Writings*, edited by Lawrence H. Simon, 315–32. Indianapolis: Hackett, 1994.

Mauss, Marcel. *The Gift: The Form and Reason for Exchange in Archaic Societies*. Translated by W. D. Halls. London: Routledge Classics, 2002.

Melina, Livio. *Building a Culture of the Family: The Language of Love*. Translated by Susan Dawson Vasquez and Stephan Kampowski. Staten Island, NY: Society of St. Paul, 2011.

———. *The Epiphany of Love: Toward a Theological Understanding of Christian Action*. Translated by Susan Dawson Vasquez and Stephan Kampowski. Grand Rapids: Eerdmans, 2010.

———, ed. *Il criterio della natura e il futuro della famiglia*. Siena: Cantagalli, 2011.

———. "Love: The Encounter with an Event." In *The Way of Love: Reflections on Pope Benedict XVI's Encyclical Deus Caritas Est*, edited by Livio Melina and Carl A. Anderson, 16–28. San Francisco: Ignatius, 2006.

———. "Pragmatic and Christological Foundations of Natural Law." In *Searching for a Universal Ethic: Multidisciplinary, Ecumenical and Interfaith Responses to the Catholic Natural Law Tradition*, edited by John Berkman and William C. Mattison III, 293–303. Grand Rapids: Eerdmans, 2014.

———. *Sharing in Christ's Virtues: For a Renewal of Moral Theology in Light of Veritatis Splendor*. Translated by William May. Washington, DC: Catholic University of America Press, 2001.

Melina, Livio, and Carl A. Anderson, eds. *The Way of Love: Reflections on Pope Benedict XVI's Encyclical Deus Caritas Est*. San Francisco: Ignatius, 2006.

Melina, Livio, José Noriega, and Juan José Pérez-Soba. *Camminare nella luce dell'amore: I fondamenti della morale cristiana*. Siena: Cantagalli, 2008.

Merleau-Ponty, Maurice. *Phenomenology of Perception*. Translated by Colin Smith. London: Routledge, 2002.

Möhler, Johann Adam. *Symbolism: or, Exposition of the Doctrinal Differences between Catholics and Protestants as Evidenced by Their Symbolic Writings*. Translated by James Burton Robertson. Vol. 2. London: Charles Dolman 1843.

Monod, Jacques. *Chance and Necessity: An Essay on the Natural Philosophy of Modern Biology*. Translated by Austryn Wainhouse. London: Collins, 1972.

Mordechai, Gordon. "Hannah Arendt on Authority: Conservatism in Education Reconsidered." In *Hannah Arendt and Education: Renewing Our Common World*, edited by Gordon Mordechai, 37–65. Boulder, CO: Westview, 2001.

Newman, John Henry. *On Consulting the Faithful in Matters of Doctrine*. Edited by John Coulson. Lanham, MD: Rowman and Littlefield, 2006.

Nietzsche, Friedrich. *The Gay Science*. Translated by J. Nauckhoff. Cambridge: Cambridge University Press, 2001.

———. *The Genealogy of Morals*. Translated by Douglas Smith. Oxford: Oxford University Press, 1998.

———. "On Truth and Lies in a Nonmoral Sense." In *The Nietzsche Reader*, edited by Keith Ansell Pearson and Duncan Large, 114–23. Oxford: Blackwell, 2006.

———. *Thus Spoke Zarathustra: A Book for Everyone and Nobody*. Translated by Graham Parkes. Oxford: Oxford University Press, 2005.

Noriega, José. *Il destino dell'eros*. Bologna: Dehoniane, 2006.

———. "Love and Reason: The Originality of the *Ordo Amoris*." *Josephinum: Journal of Theology* 17 (2010) 126–41.

Olf, Lillian Browne. *Their Name Is Pius: Portrait of Five Great Modern Popes*. Milwaukee: Bruce, 1941.

Ortega y Gasset, José. *History as a System and Other Essays toward a Philosophy of History*. Translated by Helene Weyl. New York: Norton, 1962.

Osborne, Kenan B. *The Permanent Diaconate: Its History and Place in the Sacrament of Orders*. Mahwah, NJ: Paulist, 2007.

Pérez-Soba, Juan José. "La famiglia, prima fonte del futuro della società." In *Il criterio della natura e il futuro della famiglia*, edited by Livio Melina, 31–70. Siena: Cantagalli, 2011.

———. "Love of God and Love of Neighbor." In *The Way of Love: Reflections on Pope Benedict XVI's Encyclical Deus Caritas Est*, edited by Livio Melina and Carl A. Anderson, 300–316. San Francisco: Ignatius, 2006.

Pérez-Soba, Juan José, and Stephan Kampowski. *The Gospel of the Family: Going Beyond Cardinal Kasper's Proposal in the Debate on Marriage, Civil Re-marriage, and Communion in the Church*. Translated by Michael J. Miller. San Francisco: Ignatius, 2014.

Portmann, Adolf. *Aufbruch der Lebensforschung*. Zürich: Rhein-Verlag, 1965.

———. *New Paths in Biology*. Translated by Arnold J. Pomerans. New York: Harper & Row, 1964.

The President's Council on Bioethics. *Beyond Therapy: Biotechnology and the Pursuit of Happiness*. New York: Regan, 2003.

Przywara, Erich. *Analogia Entis: Metaphysics; Original Structures and Universal Rhythm*. Translated by John R. Betz and David Bentley Hart. Grand Rapids: Eerdmans, 2014.

Ratzinger, Joseph. "Christ, Faith and the Challenge of Cultures." *L'Osservatore Romano*, English Edition, April 26, 1995, 5–8.

———. "Culture and Truth: Some Reflections on the Encyclical Letter *Fides et Ratio*." In *The Essential Pope Benedict XVI: His Central Writings and Speeches*, edited by John F. Thornton and Susan B. Varenne, 367–76. New York: HarperCollins, 2007.

———. "In Search of Peace." In *Europe: Today and Tomorrow*, 85–100. San Francisco: Ignatius, 2007.

———. *Introduction to Christianity*. Translated by J. R. Foster. San Francisco: Ignatius, 1990.

———. "The Truth of Christianity?" In *Truth and Tolerance: Christian Belief and World Religions*, translated by Henry Taylor, 138–209. San Francisco: Ignatius, 2004.

Rawls, John. *A Theory of Justice*. Cambridge, MA: Harvard University Press, 1971.

Regalado, Antonio. "Human-Animal Chimeras Are Gestating on U.S. Research Farms." *MIT Technology Review*, January 6, 2016. www.technologyreview.com/s/545106/human-animal-chimeras-are-gestating-on-us-research-farms.

Reimers, Adrian J. *Truth About the Good: Moral Norms in the Thought of John Paul II*. Naples, FL: Sapientia Press of Ave Maria University, 2010.

Ricoeur, Paul. "Approaching the Human Person." *Ethical Perspectives* 6 (1999) 45–54.

———. *Oneself as Another.* Translated by Kathleen Blamey. Chicago: University of Chicago Press, 1994.

Rorty, Richard. *Philosophy and Social Hope.* New York: Penguin, 1999.

———. "Solidarity or Objectivity"? In *Relativism: Interpretation and Confrontation,* edited by Michael Krausz, 167–83. Notre Dame: University of Notre Dame Press, 1989.

Sartre, Jean-Paul. *Being and Nothingness.* Translated by Hazel E. Barnes. New York: Washington Square, 1992.

———. *Existentialism Is a Humanism.* Translated by Carol Macomber. New Haven: Yale University Press, 2007.

———. "No Exit." In *No Exit and Three other Plays,* translated by S. Gilbert, 1–46. New York: Vintage, 1989,

Scheler, Max. "Ordo amoris." In *Selected Philosophical Essays,* translated by David R. Lachterman, 98–135. Evanston: Northwestern University Press, 1973.

———. "Repentance and Rebirth." In *On the Eternal in Man,* 33–65. New Brunswick, NJ: Transaction, 2010.

Schmitz, Kenneth L. *The Gift: Creation.* Milwaukee: Marquette University Press, 1982.

Schüssler-Fiorenza, Elisabeth. "Judging and Judgment in the New Testament Communities." In *Judgment in the Church,* edited by William Bassett and Peter Huizing, 1–8. New York: Seabury, 1977.

Scola, Angelo. *The Nuptial Mystery.* Translated by Michelle K. Borras. Grand Rapids: Eerdmans, 2005.

Secretariat of the Synod of Bishops. *Instrumentum laboris: The Vocation and Mission of the Family in the Church and the Contemporary World.* June 23, 2015.

Seneca. "Letter 66 to Lucilius." In *Selected Philosophical Letters,* translated by Brad Inwood, 15–24. Oxford: Oxford University Press, 2007.

Shapiro, Harry L., ed. *Man, Culture and Society.* Oxford: Oxford University Press, 1971.

Shub, David. *Lenin: A Biography.* New York: Penguin, 1966.

Smith, Adam. *An Inquiry into the Nature and Causes of the Wealth of Nations.* Hampshire, UK: Harriman House, 2007.

Solovyov, Vladimir. *The Justification of the Good: An Essay on Moral Philosophy.* Translated by Nathalie A. Duddington. Grand Rapids: Eerdmans, 2005.

Spaemann, Robert. *Basic Moral Concepts.* Translated by T. J. Armstrong. London: Routledge, 1989.

———. "Being and Coming to Be: What Does the Theory of Evolution Explain?" In *A Robert Spaemann Reader: Philosophical Essays on Nature, God, & the Human Person,* edited by David C. Schindler and Jeanne Heffernan Schindler, 154–69. Oxford: Oxford University Press, 2015.

———. "Gottesbeweise nach Nietzsche." In *Das unsterbliche Gerücht: Die Frage nach Gott und die Täuschung der Moderne,* 37–53. Stuttgart: Klett-Cotta, 2007.

———. *Happiness and Benevolence.* Translated by Jeremiah L. Alberg. Notre Dame: University of Notre Dame Press, 2000.

———. "Individual Actions." In *A Robert Spaemann Reader: Philosophical Essays on Nature, God, & the Human Person,* edited by David C. Schindler and Jeanne Heffernan Schindler, 139–53. Oxford: Oxford University Press, 2015.

———. *Personen: Versuche über den Unterschied zwischen "etwas" und "jemand".* Stuttgart: Klett-Cotta, 1996.

———. *Persons: The Difference between "Someone" and "Something"*. Translated by Oliver O'Donovan. Oxford: Oxford University Press, 2006.

———. "The Undying Rumor: The God Question and the Modern Delusion." In *A Robert Spaemann Reader: Philosophical Essays on Nature, God, & the Human Person*, edited by David C. Schindler and Jeanne Heffernan Schindler, 179–91. Oxford: Oxford University Press, 2015.

———. "Wahrheit und Freiheit." In *Schritte über uns hinaus: Gesammelte Reden und Aufsätze I*, 310–33. Stuttgart: Klett-Cotta, 2010.

———. *Zur Kritik der politischen Utopie*. Stuttgart: Klett, 1977.

Spaemann, Robert, and Reinhard Löw. *Natürliche Ziele: Geschichte und Wiederentdeckung des teleologischen Denkens*. Stuttgart: Klett-Cotta, 2005.

Spaemann, Robert, and Holger Zaborowski. "An Animal That Can Promise and Forgive." *Communio* 34 (2007) 511–21.

Strauss, Leo. *Natural Right and History*. Chicago: University of Chicago Press, 1965.

Taylor, Charles. *The Language Animal: The Full Shape of the Human Linguistic Capacity*. Cambridge, MA: Belknap Press of Harvard University Press, 2016.

———. "What Is Human Agency?" In vol. 1 of *Human Agency and Language: Philosophical Papers*, 15–44. Cambridge: Cambridge University Press, 1985.

Vatican Council II. *Gaudium et Spes*. Pastoral Constitution, December 8, 1965.

———. *Lumen Gentium*. Dogmatic Constitution, November 21, 1964.

Vattimo, Gianni, and René Girard. *Christianity, Truth and Weakening Faith: A Dialogue*. Edited by Pierpaolo Antonello. Translated by William McCuaig. New York: Columbia University Press, 2010.

Von Ranke, Leopold. *The Secret of World History: Selected Writings on the Art and Science of History*. Edited by Roger Wines. New York: Fordham University Press, 1981.

Waldstein, Michael. "The Common Good in St. Thomas and John Paul II." *Nova et Vetera*, English Edition, 3 (2005) 569–78.

Whitman, Walt. "Song of Myself." In *Leaves of Grass*, 25–86. Edited by Malcolm Cowley. New York: Viking Penguin, 1959.

Wojtyła, Karol. *The Acting Person*. Translated by Andrzej Potocki. Dordrecht: D. Reidel, 1979.

———. *Love and Responsibility*. Translated by H. T. Willetts. San Francisco: Ignatius, 1993.

———. "Person: Subject and Community." In *Person and Community: Selected Essays*, translated by Theresa Sandok, 219–61. New York: P. Lang, 1993.

Index